Let Ministry Teach
A Guide to Theological Reflection

Robert L. Kinast

A Liturgical Press Book

THE LITURGICAL PRESS
Collegeville, Minnesota

Cover design by Greg Becker

7   8

Library of Congress Cataloging-in-Publication Data

Kinast, Robert L.
    Let ministry teach : a guide to theological reflection / Robert L. Kinast.
        p.   cm.
        ISBN 0-8146-2374-3
        1. Pastoral theology—Field work.   2. Pastoral theology—Study and teaching.   3. Theology—Study and teaching.   4. Clergy—Training of.   5. Theology—Methodology.   I. Title.
    BV4164.5.K56   1996
    253'.01—dc20   96-21958
                                                                              CIP

To the students and colleagues
who have shared their experience, insights, and
questions with me
in theological reflection groups,

and to Judith,
who always sees something
the rest of us have overlooked.

The spirit of the
living God meets
the longing of the
human heart.
— Fred Chaddock

Contents

Introduction   vii

What Is Theological Reflection?   vii
What Makes Theological Reflection Theological?   x
How Does One Do Theological Reflection?   x
What Are the Origins of Theological Reflection?   xi

1   Where's the Theology? Ministerial Experience
    and Theological Reflection   1

2   What Am I Looking For? Describing Experiences for
    Theological Reflection   23

3   How Did I Get Here? Entering an Experience   42

4   That Reminds Me: Theological Reflection
    as Illustration   68

5   Now I Begin to See: Theological Reflection
    as Application   95

6   Is That What You Mean? Theological Reflection as
    Interpretation   123

7   Now What Do I Do? Enacting the Learning   152

Theological Reflection Bibliography   183

Introduction

Whenever I teach a course on theological reflection, I begin by asking the students why they are taking the course. The typical answers go like this: "It fits into my schedule," "My advisor said I should," "I need three more credits."

Once I asked an older student who was on sabbatical, "What about you?"

"Well, for some time now I've been hearing about theological reflection and how important it is and how practical it makes your theology. So I figured I ought to take the time to find out what this mysterious animal is all about."

This book explains what the "mysterious animal" of theological reflection is all about. It is intended for instructors and students in field education, Clinical Pastoral Education, ministry supervision, chaplain training, religious formation, and spiritual direction. With some adaptation the material can also be used by those who want to connect their faith with their daily activity, which is the heart of theological reflection.

What Is Theological Reflection?

The term *theological reflection* doesn't say much by itself. Over the past several years it has become a shorthand way of referring to many things at once. The most important thing to remember is that theological reflection refers to "learning from one's experience."

How else would a person learn? From books, from academic courses, from teachers or supervisors—in short, from someone else's experience. This is what most people think of when they hear the word *learning*. They probably picture going to school or listening to an expert or passing exams and earning a degree. Theological reflection is different.

Theological reflection deals directly with one's own experience. Of course any experience can be reflected upon theologically, but this book concentrates on the experience of ministry. The events which make up a person's ministry are the textbook for theological reflection and the minister is the instructor insofar as the minister knows what happened in his or her own experience. However, moving from "what happened" to "what it means" is not automatic. This is where the next important element in theological reflection comes into play.

Theological reflection is a method to help people learn from their experience. The method can be stated very broadly or in great detail. Very broadly the method of theological reflection consists of experience, reflection, and action. Each of these steps can be broken down in greater detail and supplemented with practical techniques as well as the learning theory underlying the whole approach. This can become very complex and unwieldy.

The present book strikes a balance between a very broad and a very detailed presentation of a theological reflection method. Each chapter describes a fundamental step in the method. The first part of each chapter briefly presents the methodological step with the help of an illustration and commentary. The second half of each chapter goes into a little more detail with longer examples and commentary. Each chapter concludes with a list of practical suggestions and a short description of the theoretical background for the main points in that chapter. The theoretical background is drawn from the school of process thought which is based on the work of Alfred North Whitehead. The theoretical section is intended for those who may ask, where did this method come from?

The third important thing to remember about theological reflection is that it is action-oriented and often change-oriented. Although the words *theological reflection* strongly suggest mental activity, the term as it is actually used includes something more and different from mere headwork. Theological reflection arises from activities such as the events of ministry. It helps a minister recognize God's role in the ministry. This recognition may entail some changes in the minister's self-awareness, outlook, motivation, and decisions. These changes become the basis for new action—the way a minister conducts the ministry and changes in the process.

All of this may seem rather overwhelming for an individual. It is. That's why theological reflection ordinarily implies a group, the fourth important thing to keep in mind. A group can help a person grasp the events of ministry more completely, analyze them, see patterns, find meanings, draw conclusions, and remain honest.

To put this another way, and to take some of the mystery out of theological reflection at the outset, it is well to keep the following points in mind:

A Group

Theological reflection works best in a small group. A group is able to see more in a given experience than an individual and a group can keep an individual from distorting or misreading an experience.

A Meaningful Experience

Some experiences are more fruitful than others: they grab one's attention; they have an impact; they hold surprises; they make a person want to discuss them. They are meaningful. These are the best experiences for theological reflection.

A Faith-Theological Perspective

A person can reflect on experience from many points of view: psychological/emotional, sociological, economic, political, legal, medical, cultural. Theological reflection helps a person look at experience in light of the person's religious beliefs and understanding of those beliefs (theology).

A Practical Outcome

Theological reflection begins with the events of one's life (ministry) and helps to shape the events which flow from them. Obviously a person cannot control everything that will happen in the future but through theological reflection a person is in a better position to guide events according to one's beliefs.

A Continuous Process

Theological reflection does not have its full effect if it is done only once in a while. It is a skill which must be practiced regularly.

What Makes Theological Reflection Theological?

The shortest answer is God. That's also the most profound and the most true answer. Theological reflection is theo-logical. Its overriding interest is God. But theological reflection is not interested in God abstractly or as proclaimed in doctrines and rituals and church policies. Theological reflection aims at something a little bit different.

It tries to help a person (or group) discover God's presence in that person's (or group's) experience. In this respect theological reflection is akin to prayer or spiritual direction (guidance, counseling). It is not satisfied with learning more about God but with leading a person more directly to encounter God. As this happens, theological reflection asks the person to consider what difference God's presence makes (the reflection stage) and what God expects as a result (the action stage). This integration of reflection and action is what ultimately makes theological reflection theological.

How Does One Do Theological Reflection?

Many methods and models exist for doing theological reflection. Each one has a different emphasis but they all agree on these basic steps:

Selecting an Experience

The events of one's life run together and overlap. They do not come neatly separated. To do theological reflection, however, a person needs to separate them in order to focus on the meaningful moments. Chapter 1 explains how to do this.

Describing an Experience

Whether reflecting privately or with a group, a person must know what happened and make the experience available for reflection. What goes into describing experience is covered in chapter 2.

Entering an Experience

In order to learn what an experience has to teach, a person must enter and relive the experience from the inside. This is discussed in chapter 3.

Learning from an Experience

This is the high point of theological reflection, in which one grasps what the experience teaches by relating it to what a person already knows and what the experience suggests is yet to be learned. How this happens is presented in chapters 4, 5, and 6.

Enacting the Learning

Until a person incorporates the learning into a pattern of living, theological reflection is not complete. Once this has been done, a person can continue the reflection process using the enactment as a new experience. Chapter 7 describes different ways of enacting one's learning.

What Are the Origins of Theological Reflection?

Before examining theological reflection more closely, it is helpful to consider why theological reflection has become so popular in recent years. Is it really a new phenomenon and, if so, is it one of those novelties that Christians are warned to avoid?

The use of the phrase "theological reflection" is quite recent. It was stimulated by the impact of liberation theology in Latin America, beginning in the 1960s. In that setting small

Christian communities would gather to reflect on their social, economic, political, and cultural lives from the perspective of their religious beliefs. These discussions started with the actual experience of the community and aimed at developing a pastoral plan to improve their lives. The whole process was often called pastoral theological reflection.

At about the same time in the United States, African Americans and women were developing their own version of liberation theology. Like their Latin American counterparts, they took seriously their own experience as the source of theological reflection and action. The experience of oppression and the quest for freedom by both groups led to a critique of their inherited theology and the articulation of a new theology.

These developments paralleled the Clinical Pastoral Education (CPE) movement in the U.S. which had been steadily gaining acceptance in the training of ministers and chaplains since its inception in the 1920s. The intent of CPE was to train ministers in the skills and personal development they needed by using their actual experience with patients. This approach was initiated in Protestant settings and was very congenial to the traditional (perhaps stereotypical) emphasis in Protestantism on personal faith and the experience of salvation.

In contrast to this emphasis, Roman Catholicism was viewed (perhaps stereotypically) as stressing doctrine and prescribed works as the path to salvation. Whether accurate or not, these characterizations point to a false opposition between experience and reflection, faith and works, personal conviction and official doctrine. The goal of theological reflection is to integrate these pairs rather than divide them. When it does so, theological reflection strengthens the practice of ministry by grounding it in its own theology while bringing theology alive by revealing it in its practical setting. In this respect theological reflection is being faithful to the very origins of Christianity.

Christianity began with an experience, the experience of Jesus—his teachings and his deeds, the impact he had on people, the feeling for life which he communicated. People talked about this experience, formed opinions about him, and even took sides. Some of those who were attracted to him became regular followers and some of those were selected by him as his intimate companions.

The culmination of this experience was his death, a shocking and traumatic event, followed by a completely unprecedented experience which his followers could scarcely describe, much less understand. Convinced that he was truly though uniquely alive after his death, they struggled for an adequate way to express their experience. The language of exaltation and resurrection served as well as it could, but the language and descriptions were meant to carry people to the experience itself.

This remains the goal of theological reflection. The starting point is experience—a full, deep, meaningful embrace of life. Reflection as a method involves recognizing what is in an event, naming it, relating it to other experiences and reflections, letting it shape the future.

The challenge of theological reflection is to keep theology in the service of experience—not just any experience, however, but the authentic experience of God's presence in our midst. To meet this challenge, theology must be critiqued by experience and experience must be critiqued by theology. The interplay is not always pleasant. Once reflection reaches a certain level of credibility and consensus, it becomes normative. Recognized as a reliable guide to the original experience, such reflection can be treated as the only guide or even equivalent to the experience itself—as if repeating that Jesus lives is the experience of his resurrection or chanting that there are three persons in the Trinity is an encounter with any one of them.

The guardians of normative theology and the institutions in which it resides can be very resistant to theological claims which come from experience, especially when they critique or interpret the established theology. It is not surprising that liberation theology, feminist theology, African American theology, pastoral theology, and other experience-based approaches have faced this resistance.

In one sense it is part of the give-and-take, search-and-find style of Christian reflection. In another sense it is unduly antagonistic and distracting. Theological reflection takes its place right in the midst of this tension. Respectful of the full range of theological resources available for reflection, mindful of the primary goal of recognizing God's presence and responding to it, theological reflection tries to weave experience and theology together into a way of life that continues the journey begun when Jesus first appeared. This handbook is offered as a companion on that journey.

1

Where's the Theology?

Ministerial Experience and Theological Reflection

A chaplain visits a person who is preparing for bypass surgery. A pastoral counselor spends an hour and a half with a married couple who are going through a stressful period. A preacher meets with a dozen members of the congregation to prepare next Sunday's sermon. A staff spends an entire meeting trying to decide how to respond to the needs of the homeless in their neighborhood. A catechist instructs a group of high school students on the meaning of the Eucharist.

These are typical ministerial experiences, the kinds of experiences that occupy a minister's time, energy, skill, and commitment. They also prompt theological reflection. Why theological reflection? The answer is that experiences like these are occasions for recognizing and acting on the presence of God, and that's what theological reflection helps a person do.

The distinctive characteristic of theological reflection is that its source material is direct human experience. Theology usually concentrates on written material like the Bible, church doctrines and classical texts, or on the principles and values which guide the moral, liturgical, and pastoral life of the Church. To be sure, this material originated in concrete human experience, but theology treats it in a generalized form. By contrast theological reflection tries to get in touch with the original form in which things happen, what is called human experience.

What Is Experience?

Experience is what happens. If that sounds simple, it is deceptively so. What happens is complex and can be viewed from different angles. For example, every human experience has a subjective and an objective side. These always go together and influence each other. The subjective side corresponds to what a person feels and does to help create the experience; the objective side corresponds to what is available for the person to feel and act upon.

For example, a visit to a homebound parishioner by a minister includes the minister's feelings, the parishioner's feelings, their verbal and nonverbal exchanges, the condition of the home, the time of day, the type of illness, the length of the visit, and many other factors, all interacting simultaneously.

In addition to subjective-objective aspects, every experience has a time dimension. It is a present event which arises out of a past and heads toward a future. Both the past and the future partially determine what the present is; the present experience cannot be fully understood apart from these dimensions. This temporal sequence is inseparable from the event itself and is another aspect of every experience.

Experience is what happens, but what happens is a flowing, indivisible, open-ended, continuous process with its subjective and objective sides emerging from the past and aiming at the future. As this is true of every experience, one might ask how a person can know which events are most useful for theological reflection?

Criteria for Selecting Experience

First of all, the experience should be specific. As in the examples above, it may be a single hospital visit or counseling session, preparation for this Sunday's sermon, a staff meeting about the homeless in this particular neighborhood, or a presentation of the Eucharist to one group of teenagers. Specificity trains a person to recognize the theological significance of the individual events which make up that person's ministry, even though this limits the general theological conclusions a person may draw from the experience.

Second, the experience should be current and personal. The purpose of theological reflection is to recognize the presence of God in the events of one's life. The most real events are the current ones. These may not be the most important events in a person's life but they are the ones that constitute a person's life right now. In this sense they have the most immediate impact and a significance all their own.

For this same reason experiences should be personal; they should be the events which actually affect a person and help shape a person's life. There is a great deal of difference between reflecting on "visits to seriously ill patients" and reflecting on one's own visit this afternoon to Mr. Hart who is facing bypass surgery. The former is anybody's experience; the latter is yours. It is real in a personal way.

Third, the experience should be important. It functions as the starting point and constant reference for theological reflection. This means it must be significant enough to stimulate reflection in the first place and substantive enough to keep theology connected to the experience throughout the reflection.

For example, responding to the needs of the homeless is an important experience for the parish staff. It stimulates them to reflect on what they are doing and leads to an identification with the parable of the Good Samaritan. After they examine the original meaning of the parable in Luke's Gospel, they begin to ask how the parable relates to their concern for the homeless. In asking this, they are keeping their theology connected to their experience.

There are no criteria which will guarantee that an important experience is selected every time. Important experiences often occur subtly, suggesting that something "more" is going on than familiar activity. It may not be immediately clear what that something more is, but it beckons for exploration. This is the impetus for theological reflection.

For example, a pastor may make or receive a dozen phone calls in a day but one of them is from a close friend in the parish who has just found out he has a malignant tumor. *That* is an important phone call. It draws the pastor into a life threatening situation, with all its implications for the parishioner, his family, the parish, his friendship with the pastor, and the pastor's sense of his own mortality.

A female youth minister may attend numerous meetings during the week, but a meeting becomes important when the parish council reports the favorable response of the congregation to her recent weekend retreat for teenagers. The parish council's affirmation of the youth minister is important because she is the first woman they have hired to fill this position and she is eager to know how her ministry is being received.

In both cases specific, current, personal experiences open up a larger world of meaning. This is how experience functions in theological reflection. It sends signals, it hints and suggests, and it invites a person to discover the theological meaning of an event. Does this happen simply because a person reflects on an experience of ministry? No. That would make theological reflection a nominal activity, concerned only with satisfying the formal requirements of a definition. Ministry is more than a name given to a certain type of activity like preaching or pastoral care. It is a promise that God's presence is especially recognizable in these actions. Theological reflection goes to work on that promise, verifying it, and drawing out its implications. Calling an experience ministry does not complete the task of theological reflection; it only begins that task.

Is it sufficient to cite a reference from the Bible or church teaching that parallels the experience? Probably not—not, that is, if the goal of theological reflection is to discover God's presence in current events, determine what difference that presence makes, and what God expects as a result. Theological reflection requires more than using theological terms. It requires living the meaning of those terms.

So what makes reflection theological? As mentioned in the introduction, the essential answer is God, and the ways God appears in the events being reflected upon. The following outline describes this more fully and suggests what a person who does theological reflection is looking for.

Theology as God-Word

Etymologically, the word theology is composed of two Greek words: God (theos) and word (logos). The relationship between God and word may be understood in at least three ways: the Word from God, the Word about God, and the Word to God.

The Word-from-God

This word is traditionally called revelation. It refers to God's original and unique self-communication to creatures. This occurs in two main forms: nature and history. In both, God communicates more often through action than utterance. The Word-from-God is deed more than speech. This gives it a pre-reflective quality that calls for interpretation once it has been discerned within the sweep of nature and the actions of men and women. Though certain events are considered definitive and unsurpassable revelations of God, the Word-from-God continues to come through creation (in its evolution and struggle for survival) and history (in its unpredictable course guided by human decisions).

A special form of the Word-from-God occurs when a person has the feeling of being taken over and used by a transcendent spiritual power. In these moments a person senses that what is happening is not under the person's control nor is it being generated by the person. It is an experience of being *in* the Word, of having the power of God flow through one's words and deeds. Because the source of this experience is God rather than the person, it is included in the Word-from-God, although it could also be listed in a category by itself.

The Word-about-God

This word is traditionally called faith. It is human self-understanding and action in light of the Word-from-God. Because it depends on the Word-from-God (and originates with it), faith is a gift from God, even though it requires human acceptance and action to become effective. The meaning of theology is most frequently identified with the Word-about-God. It takes several forms.

Confession: This is the recognition and acknowledgement of the Word-from-God as it has been discerned in nature and history. Confession declares what a community believes without including arguments or proofs for that belief. The primary expressions of this theology are the Scriptures, creeds, and doctrinal statements of believing communities. Personal witness to these communal confessions also fits in this category.

Interrogation: This is the questioning of confessions, often prompted by new experiences or new information. Interrogation is not the denial or even doubting of confessions. It is the quest for fuller comprehension which in turn can strengthen the faith and correct misunderstandings. This quest has given rise to the classic description of theology as "faith seeking understanding." The primary expressions of this theology are the disciplines of foundational and historical theology.

Investigation: This is the organizing of a coherent, intelligible, and adequate understanding of faith, often based on the results of interrogation. Investigation aims at elaborating and explaining what faith believes. The primary expression of this theology is a systematic presentation of the meaning of Scripture, creeds, doctrines, practices, and structures of faith (including the institutional Church).

The Word-to-God

In essence, this is Christian living. It refers to the response people make to the Word-from-God as understood through the Word-about-God. The primary responses take the form of prayer and worship (liturgical, sacramental, spiritual theology), moral behavior (ethics and moral theology), church life (ecclesiology, ecumenism, governance) and participation in society and culture (education, social action, practical theology).

This outline can help a person know what to look for when reflecting on experience and how to recognize where the theology is. A few examples are in order.

A woman's husband died in his mid-fifties. At the funeral a traditional bagpipe dirge was played. Some months later while vacationing with friends at the seashore and talking about the void left in her life, the woman heard a bagpipe and saw a musician practicing on the beach.

To her it was a Word-from-God that affirmed the abiding presence of her husband. She drew this conclusion because of her belief (confession) in God's fidelity, presence, and promise of everlasting life. This theological reflection in turn shaped her attitude as she began her life as a widow, a life that was in effect her Word-to-God.

A woman responsible for ministry to the elderly was beginning to question the value of her efforts and even her motives. On Easter Sunday, she was unable to attend church with her family because she had to substitute for a volunteer who didn't show up at the nursing home. She was in the back of chapel during the Easter service when a nurse wheeled a frail old man next to her and left him there.

The man was unable to hold the hymnbook, so the woman held it for him. Nor was the man able to hold his own candle during the renewal of baptismal promises, so he joined his hand to the woman's and shared her candle. Moreover, the man was unable to take the bread and cup at Communion so he asked the woman to feed him. At the end of the service he said to her, "And I hope to be with you next Easter too."

This man expressed a Word-about-God through his needs, his actions, and his comment at the end. The woman began to investigate her questions in reference to him and concluded that she had allowed administrative duties to cut her off from the elderly themselves in the same way that this man had been left in the back of chapel. She imitated his example and began asking others to help with administration so she could spend more time with the elderly.

A student was working with the Spanish-speaking members of the community, trying to get them involved in church activities. He finally succeeded in persuading one woman, a leader in the apartment building where she lived with other Hispanics, to go through the training to become a "greeter," those who visit new members of the congregation and make them feel at home.

A few weeks later, when the student inquired how her ministry was going, she told him she had not yet been asked to visit anyone. The student questioned the pastor about this and was told that the woman was divorced and therefore not suitable but, the pastor added, "I thought the training would do her some good."

The student responded to this treatment of the woman by proposing at the next church council meeting that it be stated publicly that divorced persons are not suitable as greeters. The council resisted such a restriction and refused to endorse it. The woman began visiting newcomers the following week.

The student's action was a Word-to-God, based on his theological understanding of God's acceptance and use of "the outcast." The student felt he had brought this teaching to life once again in this particular situation.

These examples illustrate the different forms theology may take in a given experience. The forms themselves only orient a person to possible theological meanings. The person must still do the theological reflection, which raises an important question.

Finding Theology or Supplying It?

Does a person simply find theological meaning within an experience, or does a person supply theological meaning to an experience, or is it a combination of both? In most instances it is a combination of both. The experience contains certain theological elements which initiate reflection. Then a person supplies a larger theological framework to name, elaborate, and enrich the theological meaning within the experience. Theological reflection thrives on this kind of creative interplay. Sometimes the experience has the lead role; sometimes the reflector does.

In the examples of the widow and the minister to the elderly, the individuals basically found theological meaning within the experience. Their reflection consisted in recognizing this theology—as a Word-from-God in the first instance and a Word-about-God in the second—and letting it guide their reactions as a Word-to-God.

In the third example the student supplied the theology in the form of a proposal to the church council. This was a Word-to-God, based upon a knowledge of the Word-from-God (God's favor to the oppressed) and elaborated through the Word-about-God (the meaning of justice)—all of which was stimulated by the experience itself.

Whether theology is found within the experience or brought to the experience, the reflection should be honest and inquisitive, respectful of both the experience and the theology. This means that questions may arise. For example, was the bagpiper on the shore merely a coincidence or really a Word-from-God, as the woman believed? What are the general criteria for deciding something like this, and how do the general criteria apply in this case?

Further reflection is often required. For example, the minister to the elderly may need to reexamine her understanding of ministry in order to make room for personal fulfillment and the use of other people's talents.

Alternative courses of action may also be considered. For example, the student may need to be more aware of how church programs actually work before recruiting people into them.

Theology as a Word-from-God, a Word-about-God, and a Word-to-God either found within, or brought to, a situation has no intrinsic limit to it. Limits are usually set by external factors such as the length of a reflection paper, the time allotted for theological discussion, the makeup of a reflection group, or the agenda items in a supervisory session. Whatever the circumstances, theological reflection should always be an honest account of where the theology is in a given experience.

The following case illustrates the points of this chapter. It presents a familiar ministerial experience: care for the dying. Death always implies theological issues. In this case the usual issues are compounded by the additional factors of AIDS, homosexuality, a hospice setting, health risks to the minister, and the attitudes of outsiders.

Dying a Good Death

Description of the Experience:

I am volunteering this year as an "emotional support person" in an AIDS program. The role of the emotional support person is to provide the client diagnosed as HIV positive, or the client diagnosed with AIDS, the opportunity to talk out their concerns, fears or anger about their illness.

My client is a thirty-six-year-old white, gay man who was diagnosed with AIDS one year ago. By the end of last summer he and his lover recognized the need for him to talk with someone about his illness. They arranged for Tom to see a psychologist as well as arranging for an emotional support person through the AIDS program. Tom had two volunteers before me but they did not work out because of their age; Tom wanted someone closer in age to himself.

My initial visits with Tom at his house were somewhat trying. He was extremely weak, his voice hardly audible, and his physical movements extremely slow. Anytime I asked a question, I would have to sit and wait for him to formulate an answer, sometimes waiting one whole minute until he answered. But the really challenging aspect of the visits was Tom's reluctance to talk at all. I think this was mostly due to his weakened condition.

In addition, Tom would cry whenever anything sentimental was being discussed, which was quite frequent. Our first two conversations were very superficial. On the third visit I detected some anger on his part regarding a certain person and asked if that person was his lover. Then Tom began to openly share about his relationship with his lover, including intimate details of their sexual relationship and their diagnoses of having AIDS.

Recently Tom was transferred to the Coming Home Hospice. The facility is beautiful, the staff very pleasant and helpful, and visiting hours are twenty-four hours a day. However, I was shocked after my first visit by the condition of the patients. I was overwhelmed at the sight of so many men around my age in one place so near death.

Tom's physical and mental condition are very poor. He is bed-ridden, is on several medications, one of which is to control hallucinations, and there is very little communication on his part. Since there is little verbal dialogue, I try to make my presence felt by such things as stroking his arm and giving him gentle head massages.

Reflection and Questions

At the seminary I talk about my "ministry" with my AIDS client. Yet with Tom, his lover, and his friends I speak of my volunteer work with Tom; I have never used the term "ministry" with them. In the gay culture, where many people feel disillusioned and rejected by institutional churches, how does a minister "minister" without jeopardizing a client relationship? Is it possible to have an effective relationship with an AIDS client if you believe that client's homosexual activity is immoral?

I have had experiences in the past of working in hospitals and nursing homes with people who are dying, but I have never before encountered such a group of younger, talented, creative people who are very near the point of death. I question not so much that death is a part of life and that it happens to young people, but why do people have to die in such a way that they are considered leprous, sinful persons? I do not want Tom to live another day. Should the medical staff be allowed to quicken his death? Should his lover, who is pained by Tom's condition, be allowed to quicken Tom's death? What does this say about my own hope as a Christian, as a minister?

I have received mixed reactions from family and friends about my working with Tom. Some have tried to persuade me to stop working with AIDS patients after Tom dies; they are afraid that I could possibly get the virus. Others have encouraged me to take Tom out to dinner. Some have implied that people like Tom are now experiencing the results of what they have brought upon themselves. How does one respond in a caring way to a variety of negative attitudes towards people with AIDS? Is it true that one "cares" for the AIDS client and "ministers" to those who turn their backs on AIDS victims?

I entitled this section "Dying a Good Death." It is my opinion that the best thing that could happen to Tom at this point is that he die peacefully and soon. How do I, whether acting as a recognized "minister" or not, help him die a good death? Isn't there something not quite right in praying to God that a person die peacefully, for doesn't that make God directly responsible for someone dying a painful, horrible death? How present, how distant is God to Tom right now? Indeed, how present, how distant am I to God in my attempt to be somewhat present to Tom in his last weeks?

Commentary

This is a sensitive account of the facts. Given the circumstances, perhaps it is even a little too objective or detached.

The role of emotional support person is described clearly but there is little indication of how the minister felt about filling this role. The minister's feelings are important for two reasons. As mentioned earlier, every experience has an objective and a subjective side which always go together and constantly influence each other. Without both, the experience is limited and so is its potential for theological reflection. At the same time strong feelings indicate where the importance of an experience lies, and this feeling of importance is a primary clue to theological meaning.

The minister describes the objective side much more fully than the subjective side. The initial visits with Tom were "somewhat trying" and demanded a lot of patience, but the minister doesn't seem too affected by Tom's frequent crying. Instead, sensing Tom's anger, the minister asks some "very blunt questions," and apparently gets the details of Tom's previous homosexual relationship, without indicating how this information affected the minister.

The first strong description of the minister's feelings is shock after the first visit to the hospice: "I was overwhelmed at the sight of so many men around my age in one place so near death." This touches on the second reason for knowing the minister's feelings. They reveal the importance of this experience for the minister, which in turn suggests where the theological meaning of this experience may be found.

The scene at the hospice multiplies and magnifies the minister's experience with Tom. There is so little activity from men who should be in the prime of their lives; there is barely any conversation, and communication is restricted to touch and gesture.

What does this say about where theology is found? What kind of God-Word is present here? Theology for the minister in this experience occurs as a Word-about-God and takes the form of interrogation. Some of the questions in the minister's reflection seem to be aimed at greater understanding. For example, some questions might be when and where to use the term ministry, how to respond to people with negative attitudes toward persons with AIDS, how to help someone die a good death, and what it means to pray to God.

Other questions seem to confront and challenge the minister's current theological understanding. For example, is it possible to minister to Tom while believing his homosexual activity is immoral? Why do people who are already suffering greatly have to die in disgrace? Is it permissible to quicken Tom's death? Where is God in all this?

These questions veer toward claiming a personal theology rather than clarifying an official church theology, symbolized perhaps by the minister's not using the term *ministry* with Tom. This suggests that the personal questions are the dominant ones in this experience.

And yet ministry does seem central in this case. Not the ministry to Tom, which the minister feels comfortable with, but the ministry as a Word-to-God, with which the minister struggles. The last sentence is revealing: "How present, or how distant am I *to God* in my attempt to be somewhat present to Tom in his last weeks?"

The answer to this question is left hanging because there is no indication of how the minister intends to investigate the questions which have been raised. Here the reflection group or supervisor can be helpful. They can ask the minister to begin answering some of these theological questions or they themselves can begin a theological discussion about them. They can ask the minister to indicate a course of investigation and request a later report on what it yields. They can suggest biblical, doctrinal, pastoral, or other resources and ask for a report after the minister has studied some of them.

Meaningful experiences often raise questions about familiar theological understandings, but there is a temptation to settle for raising questions without trying to answer them. This can also be a way to avoid uncomfortable conclusions or changes in one's ministerial style. Raising questions is not in itself theological reflection unless it initiates a process of fuller investigation, ending eventually in renewed confession of faith.

Where's the theology in this case? Initially it is in the Word-to-God, which is the ministry with Tom. That Word is largely non-verbal and implies a confession about the meaning of ministry to people like Tom—that is, it is more personal than official; it is more presence than performance; it is more conflictual than comforting.

Perhaps because the theological meaning of the experience is primarily nonverbal, it gives rise to a series of questions rather than straightforward assertions. The questions themselves probe the objective and subjective dimensions of the experience and await some ranking before investigation.

As this is done, the minister will be able to give new shape to the Word-to-God which is the ministry, perhaps even seeing the value of using the word *ministry* with Tom.

Practical Suggestions and Questions

The following points are intended for those who organize and conduct theological reflection groups. They summarize the material in this chapter and suggest how it may contribute to more fruitful theological reflection, especially when it is done in a structured setting as part of ministerial training and formation.

1. To do theological reflection, you need to have a clear idea of what theology is and therefore what is expected of those who do theological reflection.

- Do you have a clear understanding of theology and of theological reflection?
- Is this written down?
- Is it given to students and are they held accountable for it?
- Is it open to revision?

2. Theology should not be defined too narrowly (for example, as only confessions and doctrines) or limited to just one source (for example, Scripture) unless such a restriction is clearly stated for a specific purpose (for example, as part of an academic course or to improve a student's facility with that theological discipline).

- Do you restrict the sources of theology a student may use?
- Are some sources almost never used (for example, liturgy, church history, ethics)?
- What sources do you use most often?

3. Theology may not always be expressed in familiar religious language or symbols, especially when a person reproduces the actual language people used in an event.

- Do you accept theology in unconventional forms?
- How does a student demonstrate that it is theology?

4. Theology as confession is legitimate, even necessary, if theology is to be personal, but one's personal convictions are not immune from interrogation or critique.

- Do you provide time and opportunity for all three forms of the Word-about-God (confession, interrogation, investigation)?
- Do you encourage them?

5. Questions can have theological implications without ever being answered or investigated. Instead they can be glossed over with phrases like, "somehow God was present" or "that's the whole idea of redemption."

- Are students accountable for answering their own questions or those raised by others?
- Are they expected to put their answers into a systematic framework or indicate their repercussions on other areas of theology?

6. Investigation of theological issues can occur more easily if students are in programs of theological study.

- Are students encouraged to draw on current course work in doing their theological reflection?
- Are they expected to document the basis of their opinions?
- If students are not in programs of theological study, how are they helped to do theological investigation?

7. Theological reflection is akin to prayer insofar as it helps students recognize and respond to God's presence in their ministry.

- Does a student have the opportunity to describe any spiritual effects of theological reflection?
- Does the reflection group ever pray together, or pray with a student?

8. Praxis is the intended outcome of all theological reflection, especially reflection on ministry which is inherently practice oriented.

- Is praxis understood as a Word-to-God?
- Is ministerial praxis planned and carried out as part of the reflection/supervision process?
- If it is carried out, does this enactment become the basis for a new theological reflection?

9. Theology may be discovered within an experience or brought to reflection on an experience. In either case, the integrity of the experience as it actually occurred and the integrity of theology with its history of meaning should be respected.

- How is this double integrity upheld in your reflection groups?
- What are the main pitfalls and how are they recognized and avoided? For example, does a student leave the case aside once theological discussion begins rather than relating theological points to the case?

10. Theological reflection takes time.

- How much time is a student expected to spend in reflection before beginning to write?
- Is this preparation done alone or with others?
- How does a student incorporate the suggestions of others and give feedback to their input?

Theoretical Background

As mentioned in the Introduction, there are a variety of sources which have contributed to the current practice of theological reflection. There are also a number of theoretical models which lend support and clarity to this work. The primary theoretical basis for the approach to theological reflection in this book is taken from process philosophy, especially as formulated by Alfred North Whitehead. Whitehead, of course, never discussed theological reflection, but his system of thought is extremely congenial to the task of theological reflection, as I hope to show.

There are four themes in process thought which underlie the material presented in this chapter. They are (1) a process view of reality, (2) the nature of experience, (3) the presence of God in experience, and (4) the meaning of important events.

A Process View of Reality

The most distinguishing feature of a process view of reality is that all things are in process; things exist insofar as they are engaged in the activity of becoming what they will be. This is why Whitehead referred to the ultimate constituents of reality as *actual* occasions or entities. His position contrasts with the traditional (and still prevalent) view that reality is composed of substances which are already essentially constituted and act according to their specific natures. The contrast in viewpoints is often described as one of becoming rather than being, of process rather than substance.

The actual process by which any entity comes to be is thoroughly creative, i.e., the entity defines its own existence. It does this by prehending (Whitehead's term) available elements and forming them into the unique momentary occasion which is itself. These prehensions in turn constitute a network of internal relations among all actual occasions, resulting in an organic, holistic, interconnected view of reality. It is not surprising, therefore, that Whitehead described his system as a philosophy of organism.

The description of theological reflection in this book presupposes this dynamic, holistic view of reality. It is what lies behind the statement that "experience is what happens and what happens is a flowing, indivisible, open-ended, continuous process with its subjective and objective sides emerging from the past and aiming at the future." A fuller explanation of the process view of reality and of this sentence requires an explanation of the nature of experience.

Nature of Experience

Experience is what happens. This is a deceptively simple statement because what happens is a complex, largely hidden process of self creation which constitutes reality anew at each moment. The process itself consists of all the prehensions which make up the becoming of actual occasions, and these prehensions are essentially acts of feeling.

The feelings are not high-grade emotions such as joy, anger, fear, or love. They are impulses, urges, and attractions which occur in response to a felt sense of what to become and how to become in this instant, in these circumstances. This process characterizes all actual occasions from the tiniest subatomic vibration to the most complicated human thought. The feeling character of all prehensions and therefore of all becoming is what Whitehead meant by experience.

In this understanding experience is not necessarily conscious. In fact most experience is not conscious. It is, however, always affective, dynamic, and creative. Experience is affective in the sense of an impulse, an attraction, an urge rather than a complex emotion. It is dynamic in the sense that it prehends (grasps at) what it feels. It is creative in the sense that its prehensions constitute its reality.

This understanding of experience lies behind the references above to the subjective and objective sides of every experience as well as the time dimension of past-present-future. The subjective side of experience is the self-creating prehensions of every actual occasion. This is the experience of becoming which belongs uniquely and exclusively to each occasion. However, when a momentary experience of becoming is completed, it is immediately available to be prehended in a new moment of becoming. This is the objective side of experience.

No actual occasion is fully prehended in a new occasion, otherwise it would not be a new occasion but a repetition of the previous occasion. Completed actual occasions are only partially prehended along with the partial prehensions of other completed actual occasions in the creation of a new occasion. They are prehended by being felt, sensed, and taken into the experience of the new occasion. In this way completed occasions are given a future, which Whitehead called their objective immortality.

The threefold time dimension is always a factor in the generation of new experience. An occasion becomes in the present but it prehends past occasions and anticipates its own completed experience. In addition, as soon as the process is complete, the new occasion may be taken into future experiences. This same process characterizes all actual entities from the least to the greatest, from the most simple to the most complex. And yet, there are obvious differences among actual occasions. A rock is not a flower and a bird is not a human being. What accounts for the variety if the process of becoming is the same for all entities?

The answer for Whitehead is the aim of each act of becoming. Becoming is not a haphazard or arbitrary activity. It is guided by a subjective aim which lures occasions into being and gives them a goal to satisfy in their becoming. Each occasion first prehends this aim and then goes about satisfying it by the further prehensions it makes from the world around it. For many entities this process gives the appearance of inert, enduring existence. But the same creative dynamism observed in humans, animals, plants, and other living things characterizes all actual occasions.

The aims which are satisfied in every occasion give different experiences their distinctiveness. This is what allows us to name and categorize experiences as well as evaluate how well a particular instance fulfills the definition of that experience.

The experiences of ministry which are selected for theological reflection are actual occasions which more or less fulfilled their aim (consider the examples in this chapter). Each act of ministry came into being by prehending what seemed relevant for its aim. These prehensions from previous occasions (including personal history, acquired skills, and learning) were put together in a unique form which constituted that occasion of ministry.

Theological reflection is also an experience. It prehends a completed event of ministry and combines this with other relevant material (such as previous theological reflections, insights, and information) which it assembles in a unique way in order to satisfy the aim of reflecting theologically on this experience.

From this description it should be clear that experience is not one thing and reflection another. Experience characterizes all actual occasions; it is a synonym for the process of becoming. Theological reflection serves one aim; ministry serves another. But where do the aims come from? In answering this question, Whitehead becomes explicitly theological.

God's Presence in Experience

God is the originator of all aims for all actual occasions. This is what Whitehead calls the primordial nature of God. It is God envisioning all the possible, new events which could emerge out of those which have already occurred. It is what distinguishes God from all other entities. It also identifies God as the source and champion of novelty, for what God envisions and desires is new experience.

The new that God desires is not arbitrary or fanciful. It arises from the previously completed occasions which constitute creation at any given moment. God prehends all these occasions in their fullness and totality (what Whitehead calls God's consequent nature) and draws from them the aims for new occasions. In other words God elicits the best that the actual world has to offer but only what the actual world has to offer. God then shares these aims as the initiation of new experiences.

In this view God is intimately involved in and part of every experience. There is a divine dimension at the origin of all experience. The actual creation of each occasion is the work of the occasion itself, but its initiation and the consequent value of its activity is God's work. This is the divine presence in experience which theological reflection seeks to discover and articulate.

Because God is so essentially present in every occasion, a person cannot simply exclude certain events as devoid of theological meaning. Rather, a selection must be made geared toward those events which are likely to be most fruitful for theological reflection. This selection depends partly on the nature of the initial aim of the event and partly on how well the aim was satisfied. The aim of giving accurate information to an inquirer about the time of church services is not as significant for theological reflection as the aim of caring for a young man dying of AIDS, even though both aims are from God. On the other hand, remaining disengaged and impersonal while caring for an AIDS patient does not satisfy the aim of that ministry as well as overcoming personal inhibitions and sharing in the struggle of a person who wants to die with dignity. In short, some experiences are more important than others.

The Meaning of Importance

As may already be clear, in a process worldview everything is a matter of degree. The sharp dichotomies and dualisms associated with the traditional western view of reality are replaced in a process view by a holistic continuum in which everything is connected to everything else through a series of internal relationships. Thus the value of any single occasion is determined by its connection to the network of other occasions. Some occasions express in their actual constitution this larger, more encompassing system of meanings. These are the important occasions.

Whitehead contrasted importance with matter-of-fact. The two complement and require each other. Matter-of-fact refers to sheer existence, but not in the sense of self-contained existence. Nothing exists simply by itself. Everything is connected to and derived from everything else. It is this connectedness which gives rise to importance. Importance conveys a sense of how things are related; it is a glimpse of the whole which is disclosed by the particular. This is what theological reflection aims at.

The more a particular event of ministry reveals the whole to which it is connected, the more important it is. The more comprehensive a person's reflection on that event, the more important it is. For theological reflection this sense of importance may be described as a Word-from-God, a Word-about-God, and a Word-to-God. These are simply categories which alert a person to the ways a particular event can open up the larger world of theological meaning to which it belongs. Moving into that larger world of meaning is the goal of theological reflection.

In making this move, a person should not lose contact with the particular event which began the process. Otherwise theological reflection becomes isolated and disconnected, if not self serving. On the other hand, the importance of an occasion is not confined to itself. Its importance rests in the connections it manifests through its own existence. Thus theological reflection never abandons matters-of-fact but never limits itself to them either. Like reality itself, and as part of reality, theological

reflection is a dynamic experience, drawing from and con-
tributing to the collective world of other occasions which are
all together in the presence of God.

2

What Am I Looking For?

Describing Experiences for Theological Reflection

A parish minister counsels a pregnant woman who is contemplating an abortion. A lay Eucharistic minister is asked by a patient with Alzheimer's disease to hear his confession. A stock broker hosts an informal meeting of other stock brokers to discuss how their faith and spirituality affect their work. Members of a congregation discuss the role of women in the Church after Sunday services.

How should these experiences be described if they are to be used for theological reflection? The basic answer is factually.

Factual Description

A factual description is especially important when a person presents an experience to a group or supervisor for theological reflection, which is the customary format in programs of ministry training. A factual description gives those who were not part of the experience a sense of what happened. It answers the basic questions: who, what, where, when, and how?

Who was involved? In the first example, was the parish minister ordained, a professional staff person, or a volunteer? a man or a woman? married or single? Is the woman married? Does she have children?

What happened? In the second example, how did the request for confession come up? Did a family member or staff person suggest it? Did the patient with Alzheimer's know who the Eucharistic minister was or why the minister was there? What was the minister's response?

Where did the event take place? In the third example, was the meeting at the stock broker's home, at the office, at a restaurant, at a church? Was the setting deliberately chosen? How did the setting influence the discussion?

When did the event take place? In the fourth example, the discussion occurred after church services. Does this kind of discussion usually happen at that time? Did the church service itself prompt the discussion? How long did it last? Was there a desire to resume it at another time?

How did the event take place? Did the young woman make an appointment to talk about the abortion? Has the Eucharistic minister visited the Alzheimer patient before? Did the stock broker personally invite selected colleagues? Are women asking for more roles in the congregation?

A factual description provides basic information about a person's experience so that others are able to reconstruct the event more or less as it occurred. This is important because theological reflection begins with concrete experiences and seeks their theological meaning. An incomplete or inaccurate description of the experience may prevent a person from gaining the theological insight which the experience contains.

On the other hand a description need not present every detail of the event. The items included should be factual but they should also express the meaning of what happened. It's probably not important what the woman contemplating an abortion was wearing, but it is important what feelings she expressed (fear, confusion, guilt) and how she expressed them (eye contact, body posture, smiles, tears).

The initial description of an experience is not the final description. In the course of discussion other facts may be added as their relevance for theological reflection becomes apparent. For example, the Eucharistic minister may not have originally mentioned that previous visitors to the Alzheimer patient were women. When the patient saw a male minister, he may have concluded it was a priest, which is why he asked about confession.

Although the description is factual, it is not impersonal. The goal is not to present an event "objectively," as if the presenter were not part of it. This is neither possible nor desirable. Therefore the presenter's feelings, reactions, and thoughts should be included as part of the description. For example, the stockbroker may have felt anxious about inviting colleagues to discuss their faith or may have been surprised at how many accepted the invitation. These are facts which should be included in the description of the event.

What is to be avoided in the description is an interpretation of the facts. Interpretation comes later as part of the explicit reflection on the event. The description lays the foundation for subsequent interpretations. It confuses the process to introduce interpretation too soon. For example, the presenter might say, "Mary, who always advocates women's causes, started the discussion about women's roles in the Church just to get an argument started." It is a helpful fact that Mary always advocates women's causes; it is a personal judgment that her purpose was to get an argument started.

Of course, the very act of selecting certain facts and omitting others involves some degree of interpretation. It indicates what the person considers important and how the experience affected the person presenting it. This is a helpful clue to the theological meaning of the event for that person. In the course of reflection this meaning may change. What seemed important at the time of the event may be different from what seemed important when writing up the experience, and both of these may differ from what seems important while discussing the experience with others. This is a reminder that people are constantly changing; it is also an indication of the value of theological reflection.

As people move in and out of various experiences, their perspectives shift. The way they view things and what things mean to them are affected. This is a constant, dynamic, cumulative process which most people take for granted. Theological reflection helps people not to take the ordinary shifts of everyday life for granted. By requiring a person to stop, select a specific, current event, and describe it factually, the theological reflection process helps a person pay attention to what is going on, specifically to how God is present in the person's life.

Often this may only confirm what a person is already feeling; at other times it may reveal something new that hasn't been recognized by the person before. Reflection on the Sunday morning discussion about women's roles in the Church may confirm a person's conviction that women have much more to offer than the congregation realizes, whereas reflection on the visit to the Alzheimer patient may lead to a new awareness of how the lay minister participates in the priestly ministry of Jesus.

These are both valuable conclusions and they result from the way events are described. There are a number of ways to do this as the following list indicates.

Instruments for Presenting Experience

The most widely used instruments for describing experiences for theological reflection are the verbatim, the case study, the critical incident, the role play, the interview, and the journal.

The Verbatim

The verbatim is the basic instrument used in Clinical Pastoral Education (CPE) and supervised ministry involving a one-to-one relationship. It is most applicable to the ministries of pastoral care, pastoral counseling, and spiritual direction.

The strength of the verbatim is that it relies on actual conversations to teach the skills of communication (such as attentive listening and accurate responding) and of theological reflection. These verbal exchanges reveal the minister's perceptions, reactions, and style of engagement. This profile yields valuable insights into the minister, who is the prime focus of CPE supervision and theological reflection.

The primary limitation of the verbatim is that it presents only one slice of a total experience—the verbal. Nonverbal factors, which are important for both skill training and theological reflection, are not as prominent in a verbatim. In addition, a verbatim is a written document which takes on a life of its own. As a text to be analyzed, it can become a substitute for the experience rather than a description of the experience, especially in an academic setting where students are accustomed to analyzing texts.

The Case Study

The case study has a long history of use in practical disciplines such as law, business, medicine, social work, and psychotherapy. It is especially useful for decision making and pastoral planning in the ministry, and in this sense to the leadership role of ministers.

A case study helps a person develop the skills of analyzing a complex situation, taking a personal position (based on theological principles and values), and planning for its implementation. A case study that deals with group situations can expand a person's focus from one-to-one relationships and help develop the skill of working with groups. Cases can also present situations which students might not encounter in their own ministry. This not only broadens the learning experience but it can help a person anticipate situations before they occur.

On the other hand if the case does not come from a person's ministry, it violates one of the basic conditions for theological reflection—that experience should be personal. This is acceptable if such cases are used only occasionally, if they satisfy the general intent of theological reflection, and if they are well constructed. The last point is especially important because trying to do theological reflection when the facts have not been adequately presented is frustrating. This should not be pushed too far, however. One of the favorite techniques of students who do not want to do the work required by a case study is to complain that not enough information is available. If a case is well presented and used occasionally, it can be a valuable aid to theological reflection.

The Critical Incident

The critical incident is a combination of the verbatim and case study. It utilizes dialogue like the verbatim but for the purpose of focusing a situation like the case study. The critical element in the incident draws attention to what is most important in the case while keeping it grounded in its original circumstances. This can concentrate theological reflection from the outset and avoid spending time working through the entire incident in order to determine what is most significant in it. The critical incident is especially suited for examining the identity and performance style of the minister.

The primary limitation of the critical incident (shared by the verbatim) is that it can become too introspective, dwelling excessively on the minister's crises, identity, and style of ministry at the expense of other theological and ministerial concerns in the incident. The personal issues of the presenter are always important for theological reflection but they should not exclude other points of discussion.

The Role Play

The role play is widely used to simulate situations for teaching behavioral and management skills. It is most often used for one-to-one ministerial encounters, although it also lends itself to group activities.

Like the verbatim, case study, and critical incident, the role play calls upon a person's communication and analytic skills, but it adds two valuable ingredients. A role play gives immediacy to the experience and it tests a person's spontaneity and responsiveness. A role play is artificial in the sense that the situation and the participants are not the person's "real" ministry. However, while the role play is actually happening, it is a "live" event. It is not mediated or edited, as a verbatim or case study. This gives it an immediacy and realness that approximates the actual ministry more than an after-the-fact written account. These qualities enliven the experience and allow theological reflection to be more than an intellectual exercise.

In the same way a role play calls upon a person to respond spontaneously, as he or she ordinarily would, without benefit of prior reflection. This not only gives a more accurate glimpse at how the person probably ministers, but it also reveals what a person's assumptions, convictions, and values are without an opportunity to package them.

On the other hand, these benefits occur only if the role play is well designed and if the participants take seriously their roles. If there is not a well-conceived, succinct "plot" around which the role play unfolds, or if the participants are self-conscious and unable to represent their characters, the whole exercise can become distracting and interfere with the theological reflection which might result.

The Interview

The interview is a recent technique fostered by electronic recording devices and the proliferation of talk shows in the mass media. It has application to the ministry as a way of consulting with people before issuing public statements or as preparation for preaching, teaching, and pastoral decisions.

The interview helps a person develop the skill of drawing theological opinions, insights, and feelings from another person. It requires careful listening and the ability to paraphrase or summarize accurately what another person says. This is especially challenging when the interviewer does not agree with the other person's view or when opinions are stated in nontheological or inaccurate theological terms.

To obtain the desired input, an interviewer must either formulate pertinent questions ahead of time or be adept at asking questions during the interview which will lead to the desired information. In either case preparation is needed, something which the other instruments do not require to the same degree.

The primary limitation of the interview is that the questions can be restrictive, addressing only that which interests the interviewer. This may prevent a person from expressing other points which are more stimulating for theological reflection. Similarly, the interviewer has primary control of the action and can channel the responses of the interviewee along predetermined lines or rephrase statements so they fit the interviewer's theological preferences.

The Journal

The journal has become a popular tool for charting one's personal development and spiritual interpretation of daily events. As such, it is useful in spiritual direction, counseling, and programs of personal growth.

The journal utilizes a person's self-evaluation skills (similar to the critical incident) and fosters the habit of consistent reflection on the events of one's life. It also calls for the skill of synthesis as a person links journal entries together over a period of time and interprets their cumulative message. These same skills enable a person to guide others in evaluating themselves and to interpret the development of their life in relation to God's presence in it.

The primary limitation of the journal is that it can encourage a person to become too introspective, even narcissistic. Likewise, if a person shares sections of the journal with a reflection group or supervisor, they may hesitate to be critical of the person's private, perhaps even intimate, thoughts. This could inhibit the critical quality of theological reflection. In addition, members of a reflection group may be unclear about the confidentiality of what is shared.

The value of any of these instruments is how well they describe an experience and thereby stimulate theological reflection. The following critical incident presents a situation in which theology is not immediately evident. This requires the minister to bring theological values to the situation (as discussed in the last chapter) and draw out implications for praxis.

Solidarity, Empowerment, and Social Justice

Description of the Experience:

Tomas and Felipe, two refugees from Guatemala, had recently received their "papers," thereby entitling them to work. They came to me one day at the social agency where I work, ready to begin a job search.

The week before I had made a contact at a restaurant in the area. The restaurant was in the process of hiring. I talked briefly with the manager about our agency and its purpose. He seemed genuinely interested in employing refugees in the future, provided that they were legal.

My impression of the restaurant was good; the management seemed concerned about the well-being of its workers. The work was steady, the location was easily accessible by public transportation, and the manager was looking for some enthusiastic people to employ. Tomas and Felipe were enthusiastic. After waiting some weeks for their "papers," they were ready to gain steady employment. Their hope was to move eventually into an apartment of their own.

I notified the manager that there were two men at the agency who were ready to work. An interview was offered, and so Tomas, Felipe, and I arrived a week later, eager and a bit anxious. I was serving as interpreter (in my broken Spanish!) as well as *responsable* for Tomas and Felipe. We talked for some time before the manager said that he was very interested in employing Tomas and Felipe. All he needed was to see their legal papers. I swallowed hard, as I suppose Tomas and Felipe did. The papers were false.

Theological Reflection

The U.S. Catholic Bishops in their pastoral letter on the economy define social justice in the following manner: "Social justice implies that persons have an obligation to be active and productive participants in the life of society and that society has a duty to enable them to participate in this way" (ECONOMIC JUSTICE FOR ALL, no. 36). The United States denies the duty of "enabling participation" to those refugees not officially legalized or granted political asylum.

Question: how do Christians involved in refugee work progress towards the goal set by the U.S. Bishops when they are faced by the stubborn fact that society itself denies its own duty to those they seek to serve? This is the dilemma of my work at the social agency this past year.

Suggested Praxis

I suggest one possible methodology in three parts; the first part is solidarity with the "hard fact" of the poor; the second part is that of personal empowerment; and the third is one of structural empowerment. The three are not mutually exclusive, though they typically follow in the succession outlined above.

1. Solidarity is the foundational experience from which the latter two parts of the methodology emerge. Basically, the experience is one of being evangelized by the poor. We approach solidarity, according to Jon Sobrino, when we begin to realize how our own lifestyle—whether in acting or failing to act—has contributed to the injustice and oppression experienced by others. We begin not to work *for* those oppressed, but *with* them.

This significance of the experience of solidarity is obvious when we look at the common denominator to the last two dimensions of the methodology, i.e., "empowerment." Whether personal or structural, the key to the methodology is the *participation* by those oppressed. If we do not maintain a sense of empowerment in the methodology, we become guilty of practicing what Freiere calls an oppressive pedagogy.

2. Very briefly, personal empowerment has to do with those services that contribute to the dignity of the oppressed person. Depending upon the person and his/her situation, services—whether psychological, medical, educational, and occupational—may be necessary. Empowerment demands that the person enters into the process of decision-making and follow-through, whether it be occupational, medical, or educational needs.

3. Structural empowerment has to do with the efforts to challenge and reform unjust structures (e.g. current immigration law) which are at the root of the injustice the oppressed experience. Typically, a refugee is not ready for such involvement until some of his/her personal empowerment has been attained. The social agency tries to move the refugee toward a structural empowerment by their public outreach program. For the most part this program consists of refugees "telling their stories" to local Churches.

Ultimately, the agency strives toward the goal for social justice as put forth by the U.S. Bishops. The purpose is to provide the refugees with access to participation in "the system," knowing that their participation will also challenge its oppressive structures.

Commentary

Description of the Experience

The description of this incident is factual enough to give a sense of what happened. It is clear that the key players are Tomas, Felipe, the minister, and the restaurant manager. Their roles and relationships are presented matter of factly based upon the observations of the minister. The manager appears to be someone interested in hiring refugees; Tomas and Felipe are enthusiastically seeking employment but become anxious when the papers had to be produced.

The plot of the incident (Tomas and Felipe's search for employment) and its critical element (their refugee status and the need for papers) stand out against the background of pertinent facts—the necessity of employment, reasonable hiring requirements, availability of transportation, language and cultural differences.

The minister captures the drama of the incident by weaving these facts into a narrative that builds toward the critical moment. The legal status of refugees, their dependency on strangers and unfamiliar systems, their need for a job, and their anxiety about being hired are all controlled by the lifeless, impersonal papers which hold the key to this story.

The pressure is not only on Tomas and Felipe, but on the minister as well who serves as a coordinator, a translator, and a sponsor ("responsable"). These are all facts loaded with emotional force, and are appropriately included in the description. (Parenthetically, the multiple roles of the minister might remind someone in a reflection group of Barnabas mediating for Saul among the first suspicious Christians (Acts 9:26-27). This suggests that theological implications can be concurrent with the description of an experience.)

Theological Reflection

There is nothing overtly theological about this case except that it is part of the presenter's ministry. As noted in chapter 1, that alone is not sufficient to qualify as theological reflection. Consequently the minister brings a theological perspective to

the incident by analyzing it in terms of social justice as described by the U.S. Catholic Bishops.

The bishops' statement is presented as a confession (discussed in chapter 1) which is asserted without critique or even
context. Are the bishops speaking of refugees? Should illegal
aliens be considered refugees? These are questions that should
be raised during theological reflection.

The statement is used to judge subjectively United States
policy toward refugees. This is a sweeping interpretation
which may accurately express the minister's feelings, but it
gets in the way of careful theological reflection. For this asser-
tion to be developed into a credible theological reflection, it
would have to be grounded much more critically and argued
much more persuasively than it is here.

A second theological perspective is introduced with the
question, "How do Christians achieve the goal set forth by the
bishops?" This is a more objective formulation of the minister's personal dilemma which is stated at the end of the reflection section. It also raises the larger theological issue
inherent in the situation which gives the incident its importance for theological reflection. Responding to the question as
it is stated, theological reflection would take the form of a
Word-to-God (as discussed in chapter 1), specifically as a form
of social praxis. If the question were stated in terms of the
meaning of social justice for refugees or the basis for the oblig-
ations the bishops describe, then the theological reflection
would more likely take the form of a Word-about-God. The minister is consistent in responding to the question as formulated.

Suggested Praxis

The minister takes up the importance of the incident by out-
lining a method for working with the poor. How theological is
the proposed method, and does it come from the incident as
described?

1. *Solidarity:* There is ample theological support for the fundamental importance of solidarity. God's covenant with Israel,
the human incarnation of God's Word, and Jesus' identification with outcasts and sinners provide a Word-from-God

which grounds the Word-about-God from contemporaries like Sobrino and Freiere. How does such a systematic theology of solidarity with the oppressed appear in this incident, i.e., what does solidarity with Tomas and Felipe mean? Has the minister achieved this "foundational experience" of solidarity with them? Is their case an appropriate example of the theology of solidarity found in Scripture and systematic theology? These are questions which would guide a theological reflection session.

2. *Personal Empowerment:* The key word for the minister here is dignity. Persons who are otherwise victims or dependents assert their dignity when they are able to feel their own power and act on it. Again there is ample support for this definition in the example of Jesus and in current pastoral literature. The question remains, however, were Tomas and Felipe empowered? How did they enter the "decision-making and follow-through process" regarding their job search? Did having false papers empower them?

3. *Structural Empowerment:* This is the ultimate goal of action for social justice. Certainly the prophetic tradition in Scripture and history is relevant here. On this point the minister does make an explicit connection with the case by describing how the refugees tell their stories to the local parishes. At first this may seem a weak response to the influence of unjust structures. However, further theological reflection could show how storytelling is linked to the power of the Word whereby it takes on greater theological and practical significance. When the Word-from-God is reiterated in today's world and proclaimed by those who experience it as such (Tomas and Felipe?), it shares in the power of the Word itself. This is the same Word which brought creation into being and periodically changed the course of history. Is that what the refugees' "telling their stories" is expected to accomplish? Could more be done to transform their experience into effective, theologically-grounded praxis? This is a fitting topic for discussion by the reflection group.

This critical incident is important not only for the ministry but also for theological reflection. The questions which the minister raises come out of the incident itself but have implications for many other situations. This larger impact is what makes the event important.

The minister's theological reflection begins as a confession in language taken over from the U.S. Catholic bishops. The questions which are raised do not interrogate the confession but investigate its implications. The risk is that the original incident, so well described, will be left behind as the minister reflects theologically on solidarity and empowerment. To some degree this occurs. The three steps of the proposed methodology are not related to the incident for critique or refinement or even illustration. Only at the end is there a reference to the work of the social agency and it is stated in very general terms (the public outreach program of refugees telling their stories).

Losing contact with the originating experience is more likely to occur when theology is brought to a situation, as in this case. However, it is always possible that this will occur, even when an experience has been well described.

Practical Suggestions and Questions

The following points review the material in this chapter and offer suggestions for improving the description of experiences used for theological reflection.

1. The description of an event for theological reflection should be factual.

- Do you explain the importance of a factual description to your students?
- Do you give students a format to follow in describing their experience (e.g., who, what, where, when, how)?
- Do you give students examples of good descriptions which they can use as a model for their own?

2. A factual description is not necessarily an impersonal description.

- Are students encouraged to include their observations and personal feelings as part of the description?
- Are students taught to distinguish between their observations and feelings and their interpretations or judgments?

3. Additional facts can be added to the description as they are needed during the theological reflection.

- Do you provide the opportunity for clarification of facts at the beginning of a reflection session?
- Are students encouraged to rewrite their descriptions in light of the need for additional or different information?
- Do you note whether a student's description is ordinarily adequate or consistently incomplete?

4. The description of experience can be given through a variety of instruments.

- Do you include a variety of instruments?
- Are students encouraged or required to use different instruments?
- Do you explain new instruments before they are used and give examples of them?

5. Each instrument has its strengths and limits.

- Are you aware of the strengths and limits of each instrument you use?
- Are students free to choose the instrument they think is most appropriate for the experience they present?
- Does the nature of the experience and the goal of the reflection determine the selection of instrument?

6. Theological reflection should remain connected to the facts of the experience as described.

- Do you ask students to show this connection?
- Is the interplay between concrete particulars and general themes balanced?

Theoretical Background

The material in this chapter on the description of events relies on the following concepts in process thought: (1) the importance of empirical data; (2) the function of symbolic reference; and (3) the danger of misplaced concreteness.

The Importance of Empirical Data

Process thought is at home in the school of philosophy known as British empiricism. According to this school, the starting point

for understanding reality are "the stubborn, hard facts" of common sense experience. There is much debate among empiricists
about whether these facts are actually knowable and what criteria guide and validate the knowing process, but all empiricists
stand together against idealists who regard empirical facts as the
expression of *a priori* and more primary reality—mind or reason
or thought or idea.

Clearly, the issue at stake is not one of either/or since any
comprehensive philosophy must take account of both empirical facts and rational thought. Rather, it is a question of their
combination or interaction. For Whitehead, whose quest was
for a coherent, logical, and adequate explanation of the data revealed by modern physics, the starting point is always the
basic facts. They are the key to intelligibility but their meaning
is not self-evident. In fact, empirical data can be very deceptive.

The primary access of human beings to empirical facts is
through the physical senses. However, the data of the senses
give the misleading impression that each thing is a self-contained entity and that the most important fact about each entity is what the senses perceive, namely its size, shape, color,
weight, location, movement, etc. This is deceptive. These may
be the most obvious and immediate features of sense data but
they are not for that reason the most important features of the
objects themselves. Their importance lies, as pointed out in the
last chapter, in their connectedness, in what they reveal about
the nature of reality as a whole.

It is this larger picture which the inquiring mind seeks, but
the only access to it is through the data of individual occasions. This is a tedious process, for the mind wants to leap
ahead to generalizations and abstractions. It takes a deliberate
effort and discipline to keep the mind focused on the data and
to keep measuring speculative conclusions by their coherence
with the data.

On the other hand philosophical interest is not centered on
empirical facts for their own sake. This would result in an excessively narrow and deficient view of reality. Empirical interest is for the sake of speculative reason, for an inclusive view
of reality which the empirical data make possible.

Theological reflection approaches the data of experience

with the same outlook. Its ultimate goal is to formulate the theological meaning of a given experience (and, beyond that, the theological meaning of all actual experience, insofar as this is possible). By definition, this meaning goes beyond the factual account of the experience itself even though this larger meaning is available only through the facts of the event. This is the primary reason for insisting on a factual description of the events reflected upon. The facts reveal the meaning; they speak for themselves, but what they have to say is more than themselves, for the facts reveal meaning not within the limits of their own actuality but as a symbolic reference to the larger reality which they share and partially concretize.

Symbolic Reference

The larger dimension of every finite occasion, the connection of a particular empirical fact to the network of other actualities is its symbolic reference. Every fact points beyond itself by simply being itself. The interest of theological reflection, as of all speculative thought, is in "the beyond" to which facts point.

It takes a symbolic turn of the mind to recognize and articulate the larger whole which facts disclose. This already begins with the very description of events, which is something different from the event or its meaning. It is a symbolic account which creates the possibility for meaning to appear. For example, the description of Tomas and Felipe earlier in this chapter represents these men; it highlights certain features and omits others. It is a creative mediation between mere matters-of-fact about them and their importance in this experience.

What the mind does with the sense data it receives is convert it, almost instantly, into symbolic forms that in effect recreate the world and condition the way a person perceives it and therefore functions in it. If the minister perceives the restaurant manager as "genuinely interested in employing refugees," this is a complex symbolic interpretation which prompts the minister to recommend Tomas and Felipe for employment. Perception gives rise to reflection; reflection leads to action; action (praxis) flows from reflection.

This process of symbolically interpreting and interacting with one's world does not begin from scratch each time. In fact a person learns the symbolic reference of basic facts simultaneously with the facts themselves. This points to the social or communal construction of reality which conditions each individual and into which a person is socialized. For example, Tomas and Felipe learn not only that papers are needed; they also learn the importance of these papers, what they make possible, and what they represent. This meaning distinguishes these papers from other papers and symbolizes the social reality into which Tomas and Felipe are moving.

To interpret the meaning of these papers differently (as the minister does, seeing them as a denial of the country's duty to enable refugees to participate) and to act on that different meaning is also a symbolic reflection. Because it is not in harmony with the prevailing meaning, it creates tension and calls for critical reflection. This illustrates how the same situation can give rise to different interpretations and different courses of action. Part of the task of critical reflection is to sort through these options, relate them to a larger frame of reference, and make decisions about the meaning and praxis called for by the situation.

Theological reflection is a deliberate, concentrated exercise of symbolic reference. It refers the hard data of an event to the symbolic world of theological meaning and helps a person sort through the possible connections which the experience allows. This is not an exercise in fantasy or make-believe. It is an extension of the fundamental urge of all human knowing channeled in the specific direction of theological meaning. Like all human knowing, however, theological reflection can substitute its concepts for the reality they symbolically represent.

Misplaced Concreteness

One of the greatest risks inherent in any form of reflection is misplaced concreteness. This means that a person's ideas about something are substituted for the reality itself and then treated as if they were real. This fallacy is especially prevalent in idealistic, rationalistic philosophies, something to which Whitehead was especially sensitive. Once the idea is treated as the reality it represents, the symbolic process breaks down and the grounding in reality is lost.

Symbolic reference is an interpretation of the world of sense data but it is not a substitute for that world. All reflection should be tested and measured by the reality from which it comes. Suppose the minister who is helping Tomas and Felipe fixes on the idea of empowerment and its generic definition drawn from authoritative sources (which is how the reflection was actually presented). Unless the idea of empowerment is explicitly related to the concrete circumstances of Tomas and Felipe, its reality can be misplaced and the attempt to deceive the restaurant manager can result in greater disempowerment for Tomas and Felipe.

The fallacy of misplaced concreteness is a constant temptation for those who do theological reflection. They can treat theological concepts and constructs as if they are the reality they represent, forgetting their origins in human experience and the need to test their adequacy in current experience. One of the clearest signs that this is happening is when a person begins a reflection with a concrete event and then abandons the event once theological reflection begins. It is as if the event were merely a prod for theological reflection to assume its own, independent existence.

In a process view theological reflection is genetically tied to concrete events and every event evaluates the theological meaning previously articulated. The key to achieving this and avoiding misplaced concreteness is to describe events factually.

3

How Did I Get Here?

Entering an Experience

Describing an experience is an essential first step in theological reflection. The purpose of the description is to re-present the event and make it available to those who are going to reflect on it. In order for them to learn from the experience, it is important that they make the experience their own; that is, they must enter it. The present chapter describes various ways to do this.

To concretize the process of entering an experience, and to become acquainted with reflecting theologically on a verbatim, consider the following ministerial experience.

A Pastoral Care Verbatim

Keith (K) is a twenty-five year old graduate student in the music and fine arts department at a local college. He is an excellent musician, has composed a number of songs, and is very active in the liturgies on campus. Before beginning graduate studies, he spent one year in a pre-theology program at the regional seminary but decided not to go on for ordination. He hopes to become a church music/liturgy director.

Last summer, Keith went to Europe on a study tour. While there, he became ill and has been slow to recover. At midterm Keith made an appointment to see me, the campus minister (CM). He arrived on time, as usual, and after initial pleasantries, I asked him how he was feeling.

Verbatim

K1	That's what I want to talk to you about.
CM1	OK (not sure of what was coming).
K2	I don't know how to say this. I haven't told anyone else yet. I just found out myself yesterday. (pause) I'm going to die.
CM2	(Feeling stunned and concerned) What do you mean you're going to die?
K3	I have AIDS.
CM3	AIDS? Are you sure?
K4	I've done all the tests. Twice. The doctor gave me the results yesterday. It's definite.
CM4	Oh, Keith, I'm so sorry. I just don't know what to say.
K5	I know. There really isn't anything to say.
CM5	(After a few moments of silence) How are you feeling?
K6	You name it, I'm feeling it. I've been all over the map emotionally. I don't even know where to begin.
CM6	I'm sure you don't. Why not tell me what you're feeling right now.
K7	Scared.
CM7	Of dying?
K8	Of suffering. And of the suffering I'll cause others. I have AIDS because I'm gay. Nobody knows about that—my family, my teachers, the community here, you. At least, I haven't told anyone.
CM8	You're right, Keith. I didn't know. (Short pause) You really are carrying a lot, aren't you?
K9	And it hasn't even begun yet.
CM9	What do you mean?
K10	The suffering. The embarrassment. The costs. The changes. All of it. I feel like I'm sitting on a building watching my life come to a corner and I see everything waiting around that corner.
CM10	What would you like to do, Keith, as you look down on what's about to happen?
K11	Take a detour. Stop the car. Anything but turn that corner.

CM11   Can you do any of those things?

K12   No, not really. I've got to go ahead.

CM12   How would you like to turn the corner, Keith? How would you like to deal with what's there?

K13   With dignity.

CM13   What would that mean, regarding any one of the things you've mentioned—the suffering, the embarrassment?

K14   Right now, the hardest thing is telling everybody how I got AIDS.

CM14   You anticipate it will be hard telling people you're homosexual?

K15   Not hard telling them—they'll probably figure it out when they hear I have AIDS. I mean, there are only two ways to get it, right?

CM15   But that isn't what you want, is it, for people to find out you have AIDS and draw their own conclusions?

K16   Right.

CM16   What *do* you want, Keith? How would you like to tell people about this with dignity?

K17   I don't know, but what I want is to be able to look people in the eye and say, "I am who I am. I made my choices and this is what happened."

CM17   And that's it? That's all you want to say?

K18   Well, I'm not going to say I'm sorry, I wish I hadn't done it, don't any of you take this chance. I'm not going to give a sermon or ask forgiveness.

CM18   No, I wouldn't expect you to, knowing you as I do, Keith. But how would you like people to respond to you when you tell them?

K19   To accept me. To understand me. To stay with me.

CM19   Are you scared they won't?

K20   (Beginning to cry) Yes. I am afraid of that. I don't want to be alone.

CM20   (Taking Keith's hand, then embracing him). You're not, Keith. You're not.

As mentioned in chapter 2, a verbatim concentrates on dialogue. It usually begins with a summary of pertinent facts and then reproduces the narrative more or less as it took place. Accuracy is important but need not be slavishly reproduced because the primary goal is to let the presenter share his or her experience of the ministry. This includes theological issues which may have arisen in the course of the conversation as well as issues which occur to the presenter later when recalling and describing it.

Those who are reflecting on the experience with the presenter should try to enter into it and make it their own. This will enable them to learn what this episode is teaching "from the inside." It will also help them to take the episode seriously as a source of theology and not just as a prelude to general theological discussion.

How can a person enter the experience of someone else? More specifically, how can a person enter the experience of the campus minister in the preceding verbatim? In general, there are three entry points for reflection, corresponding to the three main components of any event: the players, the plot, and the place. An individual doesn't have to follow any particular order or utilize all three. In a group reflection, it is likely that at least one person will be attracted to each of the entry points.

The Players

The players are those who are directly involved in the event. In the verbatim, the key players are Keith and the campus minister (although others are mentioned in the course of the dialogue). The players do not have equal roles. One person usually has a dominant role and the others have subordinate roles. The dominant role is the one which defines the relationship of everyone else. In this case Keith is the dominant player to whom everyone else in the verbatim is related, including the doctor (K4), "others" (K8, 14), and the campus minister. When entering an experience through the players, a person should pay attention to the one who has the dominant role and those who have subordinate roles.

After identifying the players, a person should examine how they actually relate to one another, i.e., what are their roles, their expectations, their feelings, their influence? For example, Keith seems to relate to the campus minister not as a counselor or even a church official (who might judge his moral state) but as a friend in Keith's faith community. Keith is worried about the community's reaction to him and may be using the campus minister to test his anxiety (a part of what he senses waiting for him "around that corner," K10).

If this is true, then already at this point the experience suggests a theological lesson. Keith relates to the campus minister as a representative of the community but he does this from his own perspective, in order to satisfy his needs. Is this what it means for a minister to represent a faith community? Is this consistent with the campus minister's self-image? If not, is it possible that Keith's action could broaden the self-image which the campus minister had before this encounter? These are the kinds of theological questions a verbatim can raise; they should be noted at this stage for fuller discussion later.

The Plot

The plot refers to the issues or values which are at stake in the event. This gives the experience its dramatic quality and intensity. Important events usually have several plots. For example, the verbatim with Keith touches on the issues of death (K2), AIDS (K3), fear (K7), helplessness (K10 and 20), human dignity (K13 and 17), morality and guilt (K18), and acceptance (K19). These are important issues which people face in many different situations. Keith's experience provides one perspective on these larger themes and warrants further reflection.

When entering an experience through the plot, it is important to identify the dominant issue which ties the others together. The dominant issue usually recurs in the course of the narrative and is often expressed through images or symbolic language. In the case of Keith, the dominant issue seems to be his fear of rejection. This shows up often (K2, 5, 7–10, 11–13, 15, 17–20) and it draws together the subplots—the fact that he has AIDS and faces death from it, that he is an active homosexual, that this probably violates the morality of those from whom he seeks acceptance.

Keith expresses his fear and uncertainty symbolically. He's been "all over the map emotionally" (K6) and he feels like he's sitting on a building watching his life come to a corner which he'd like to avoid by taking a detour (K10 and 11). These travel images suggest an uncertain, fearful journey.

There is a theological dimension here also. Keith's fear, his desire for acceptance, and his anxiety about the future are basic themes in the story of salvation. It is not yet clear how Keith's situation relates to this general theme or what light the theology of salvation may shed on his experience, but the verbatim is restating this basic plot of salvation history in its own terms.

The Place

The place is the setting in which an event occurs. It includes not just the physical space but all the factors which interact to create the experience. The place is a dynamic network of forces rather than a lifeless or empty stage. However, in comparison with the appeal of the players or the drama of the plot, the influence of the place may easily be overlooked. One way to avoid this is to include social analysis in every theological reflection.

Social analysis is a tool for examining any situation in order to uncover the elements which structure it to be the way it is. These elements are not always obvious and often require special attention. The main categories of social analysis, as they appear in the verbatim with Keith, are:

> *economic:* this concerns finances, costs, monetary resources (for example, in K10 the cost of AIDS care is mentioned)
>
> *political:* this refers to the meaning and use of power or control, most often by the government but not only in that context (in K17, Keith speaks of the ability to look people in the eye and assert, "I am who I am.")
>
> *cultural:* these are symbolic, colloquial, idiomatic expressions of meaning in the culture which people typically use (for example, in K6 Keith uses a familiar image to describe himself as "all over the map" emotionally)
>
> *social:* this pertains to the roles, relationships, systems, and status which regulate the interactions among people (in K8 Keith refers to his relations with family, teachers, and friends; in K14 he anticipates having to tell everybody about his condition)

> *gender:* refers to male and female relationships, including homosexuality (for example, when Keith acknowledges in K8 "I'm gay.")
>
> *generational:* this covers life stages, human rights, needs, tendencies, desires (in K19 Keith expresses the desire and need for acceptance, understanding, presence from others).

These categories can help identify the dominant factors which shape the setting of the experience. The dominant factors situate the plot and the players within a larger social context.

For example, the dominant factor for Keith seems to be the social attitude toward homosexuals with AIDS. A large part of Keith's fear of rejection comes from his assumption that most people feel negative toward homosexuals (K8) and perhaps for that reason less compassionate towards homosexuals with AIDS. His determined, almost defiant, intent to retain his dignity (K13) and not make apologies for his actions (K17 and 18) seems to be aimed at this social attitude more than at the campus minister.

This suggests that the place in this episode has its own theological meaning. Society's attitude toward and treatment of homosexuals, its response to AIDS, its tendency to form moral judgments, its assessment of human dignity have theological implications. They may not be stated in explicit theological language, but they are based on a qualitative view of life from which standards are derived. To this extent at least, they share the same genre as confessional religious statements and may warrant closer study as part of the theological reflection on this verbatim.

Entering another person's experience (or one's own in a private reflection) is a creative, adventurous undertaking. It can be aided by knowing how to use the clues which the experience provides.

Clues Along the Way

The goal of theological reflection is to recognize the divine presence in human experience. The divine presence is rarely self-evident, which is demonstrated by John the Baptist's need to point out Jesus to his two disciples (John 1:29-34). Theological reflectors may not always have someone like John the Baptizer at hand, but the experience itself, as the medium of divine presence, leaves its own natural clues. The most common of these are linguistic images, physical objects, and spontaneous gestures.

Linguistic Images

All language has a theological character insofar as it is a human participation in God's original Word. Because God's Word is essentially creative, the language that participates most closely in God's Word is language that creates, and the most creative form of human language is imaginative.

People use images to express what is important to them, what they feel acutely, what impacts their lives keenly. Not all images open a door directly onto God's presence, but if God's presence is being felt, if it is a significant part of a person's experience, it will come to expression through images.

Of course, language has a life of its own. It is not always under the conscious control of the person speaking. This is especially true for images which contain meanings that are sometimes as much a revelation to the speaker as to the hearer. That's why theological reflection pays special attention to the images people use in their conversations.

Physical Objects

Objects are the products of God's ongoing creativity which has been shared in a special way with human beings. Not all objects reflect the divine artistry or purposefulness to the same degree, but all objects ultimately derive from the original divine impulse to create. They help to construct a world which expresses and engages its maker. This is their inherent theological dimension.

The way people use objects is a clue to where and how God is present in their experience. Likewise the way people misuse objects is a clue to where and how God is absent in their experience. Objects are not just lifeless things to be manipulated for an extrinsic purpose. They reveal or resist the meaning of God in the lives of the people who use them. That's why theological reflection pays attention to the use of objects.

Spontaneous Gestures

When God breathed life into the first earth creature, it was a gesture, an external demonstration of an internal reality. Stirred by the very breath of God, humans imitate this divine activity in their own gestures, especially the spontaneous gestures that occur without planning or calculation. These are often the manifestation of God's Spirit breathing as she wills. For this reason a person using a particular gesture may be just as surprised by it as an observer is and equally unable to explain its origin or significance.

Sometimes gestures are intentional, meant to convey what words or objects cannot. Such gestures embody meanings which might otherwise take many words or objects to express. Whether spontaneous or planned, gestures are the outcome of an inner movement, which blends many elements together and gives them an external form. This is why theological reflection pays attention to people's gestures as a clue to the theological meaning of their experience.

The clues which help a person enter an experience in order to do theological reflection occur within the experience itself. They should not be artificially imposed or inserted. On the other hand, these clues are often small, subtle, and simple. They can be easily overlooked while searching for a large, comprehensive meaning.

The following examples of ministerial experience illustrate how a person can enter an experience following the lead of images, objects, and gestures. The accounts come from ministers working in a variety of situations. The clues and meanings pointed out in the commentary are surely not the only ones and may not even be the most instructive ones. This is a reminder that the goal of theological reflection is not to reduce an experience to just one meaning but to expose everything it has to teach.

David's Bicycle

Last September I began working at Horizon Community Center for alcohol and drug recovery. Horizon Center is a county-funded, nonresidential program for individuals, families, and the community affected by alcohol and other drug related problems. Working from the social model rather than the medical model, this is done primarily through process groups (therapy), providing information necessary for diagnosis, interviews and treatment, individual sessions, and community education. Because it is a county-funded program using a sliding scale method of payment, the Center attracts mostly lower-income people who cannot afford private treatment.

Although my primary function at the Center is as an intern cofacilitator for two process groups, I spend my time between supervision and facilitating in the front room, answering phones and taking care of visitors. It was during this time that I met David, a six-year-old Filipino who had been coming to the Wednesday afternoon Children of Alcoholics (COA) group.

He had been absent for the last two weeks and arrived to find that the COA group had ended the week before because the facilitator had unexpectedly quit the Center. The person who had brought David had already left and, since no one else was available, I was given the job of entertaining David for an hour until his uncle returned.

David's only question to me was "What happened to Janet?" (the facilitator who left). As I tried to explain, I was puzzled by his blank stare and lack of any further interest in that matter. I asked him about his family, but he didn't want to talk about them. After running out of possible topics of conversation without much success, I found some paper and crayons for him and left him alone.

Toward the end of the hour I noticed that one of the things he drew was a picture of a house with a bicycle in front. When I asked him if it was his house and bike, he replied rather matter-of-factly that it was, but that his father (who no longer lived with him) had come by two weeks ago and had taken the bike. That's all he would say.

After David left, I talked to one of the supervisors at the Center who knew him. She said that David's father was an addict who had abandoned the family about a year ago. David's mother is an active alcoholic/addict. When the police came looking for her a month ago, she jumped out the window and ran away, abandoning David. He is now living with an aunt and uncle.

Commentary

This incident occurs in between the minister's main work of supervising and facilitating. It is a reminder that sometimes the most revealing experiences occur in the "off" moments, when nothing is supposed to happen.

David is the key player who provides entry into the theological meaning of this experience. What are the clues he leaves? There don't seem to be any linguistic images, although David's question, "What happened to Janet?" is intriguing. From the background given above, it may suggest that David feels that things "happen" to people in his life, specifically, that they disappear.

The first real clue is a gesture: "I was puzzled by his blank stare." This obviously caught the minister's attention, as well it should. A blank stare from a six-year-old child is not expected. A blank stare suggests emptiness, vacancy, a void where there should be fullness, excitement, vitality. These associations trigger theological parallels: the great void before God began creating, the barren desert before Israel's exodus, the empty tomb after Jesus' resurrection.

Against this theological backdrop, a blank stare may be taken as a prelude to God's intervention. If so, how might God act in David's case? What role might the minister play in carrying out God's action? These would be suitable questions to discuss during a theological reflection on this incident.

There is a second clue. It is a combination gesture, image, and object—the bicycle in front of the house which David drew. It is tempting to slide into an amateur psychoanalysis of this drawing but theological reflection serves a different purpose in examining this clue.

The bicycle belongs to David. Bikes are a familiar symbol of childhood representing innocent fun, free movement, playful activity. All this has been taken away from him. He is like a miniature Adam expelled from the garden of Eden, except that he is not culpable for his fate. He does not now possess the objects he desires (and what they symbolize) but he retains his desire for them through his imagination. This is a spiritual gift, a stirring of God's own creativity in David and a promise of redemption.

There may not be another opportunity for the minister to visit with David, but if there were, it would be appropriate to explore his imagination, reinforce it, and see what can be done to begin realizing what he envisions. In any event David's blank stare and crayon bike are clues to the theological meaning of this episode.

Granny Cody

Her face looked like the map of Argentina carved in leather. Every so often she'd lean over to her right side, bring two fingers to her lips, and spit out a wad of tobacco juice onto the grass. Most evenings after supper she would be sitting on her porch. In her weathered, wicker chair, she'd be tilting back against the wall. Her feet'd be resting on the bottom rung. It wasn't much of a chair. It wasn't much of a porch for that matter. Just room enough for another chair or two and a welcome mat that was close to wearing out its own welcome. The porch wasn't much different from the rest of the house.

House? It was a glorified three-room shack, perched on a tiny plot of land at the top of the holler. But it was her land, her house, her porch. And she was damn proud of it. As well she should be.

Each day, the van would pull up in front of her house and drop her off after an afternoon of lunch and gossip at the senior citizens' center. As she gingerly descended the ramp, her closest companion would wait for her on the walk. His stump of a cat's tail would flutter as he greeted her. She'd stoop down to pet him, and he'd turn horizontal cartwheels. "Rollie, Rollie, Rollie," she'd say. She'd give him whatever food she whisked out of the center. After he feasted, he'd jump on her lap and stick his head over her ample, sagging breasts and poke his nose in her face. She'd scratch between his ears and coo, "Love me, Tom. Love me."

Love me. That's what Granny wanted. That's what I desire. That's what we all need. Why is loving ourselves so difficult? Methinks that each of us, to himself or herself, needs to coo in Granny's words, "Love me."

My cousin lost her mother in June after a five-year battle with emphysema. A month after the funeral, my cousin came to visit for a long weekend of rest and contemplation. I brought her over to Granny's. We sat on the porch and chatted for a while. When we had to head back for supper, Granny wanted to know when she was leaving. "On Tuesday," she said. Granny asked her, "What's your hurry? Places worth livin' in shouldn't be left too soon."

What's your hurry? I've found myself wondering that these past months. Don't you derive as much gratification from being as from doing? Why do you avoid hanging out with God, especially when you find that you love it, that when you do it, it's the most important part of your life?

Commentary

This minister has a flair for describing an experience very creatively. The theological reflection that accompanies each vignette shows a comparable ability to find theological meaning in the ordinary details and language of Granny's life.

Objects

There is an obvious bonding of Granny with her possessions. Her objects express who she is, a woman of the land whose home is open for visitors and conversation. One can almost hear her answering a stranger the way Jesus answered the disciples when they asked where he stayed: "Come and see." One might also imagine this minister sitting at Granny's feet the way Mary sat at Jesus' feet, absorbing what he had to say.

Gesture

Granny's affection for the tomcat, Rollie, is a gesture with deep meaning for the minister. It is not difficult to draw theological parallels between Granny and a biblical image of God. Her arrival brings excitement to Rollie; she calls him by name and feeds him, indeed gives him a "feast." Then he snuggles close to this primal source of life and is loved. This scene brings alive Jesus' words: "Look at the birds of the air (and cats of the holler). Your Father (Mother) in heaven takes care of them and are you not more important than they?" (Matt 6:26)

Image

Granny wonders why the minister's cousin is in a hurry to leave the area. Granny can't hurry, and probably never did. There is always too much to take in, to feel, to linger with. She has become so intimate with her world that she can't imagine rushing through it or leaving a worthwhile place. Granny's way of not hurrying through life may be just the clue that reveals the meaning of time in heaven, or the time on earth that deserves to be called sacred.

Sixto and the Hope for Justice

Sixto, twenty-nine, has a wife and two children and comes from one of the rural communities near the border of Peru and Bolivia where I have been working. One evening early in September he was returning from Bolivia where he had sold a number of mules on behalf of members of his extended family. On the way he was robbed of a large sum of money by four members of the border police.

Through the night they tortured him at their house and police station trying to get a "confession" that would justify their keeping his money and would get him to keep quiet. Finally they put a mattress over him and shot him so they could say he was shot trying to escape. He moved at the last minute and instead of hitting him in the heart, they hit his shoulder, which was nearly destroyed.

Somebody got scared that things had gone too far and they would be found out, as many knew about it by this time. So they took him to the local hospital. Someone notified a woman churchworker who went immediately to stand guard by him and take him to the hospital in Punto, two hours away. She also kept him from being taken to the police hospital where they could cover it all up. Lawyers were immediately notified at the Peace and Justice Office of the Church, and they began to document the case.

We have been pressing the legal case on behalf of Sixto since then. For a time the four police were in jail, something that practically never happens, and the two officers in charge that night are still in jail. The case will go on for a long time. In pressing the case, we hope to put the brakes on police violence which has been on the increase, and defend the rights of the rural poor who rarely have any hope of justice or defense in such situations.

Sixto was operated on at the hospital and, by the grace of God, is recovering much of the use of his arm. His courage has allowed him to be very clear in his testimony in the case.

Commentary

The narration of this incident—with its social justice theme, and its economic, political, cultural, and military oppression subplots—is very factual. What kind of theological reflection does this experience make possible? Where are the clues?

Object

A significant object in this narrative is the mattress. A mattress ordinarily suggests rest, sleep, refreshment, lovemaking, bonding, the generation of new life, all of which are positive human experiences which are part of God's creation. In this case the use of a mattress contradicts these values, disguising an attempted murder to hide a robbery.

Sometimes the misuse of objects "awakens" us to the reality around us, sharpens our vision (as when we are rested), and renews our energy to act (as after a good night's sleep). In this case the mattress may also recall the time Jesus said he had nowhere to lay his head, a theological metaphor for the plight of Sixto and the villagers.

Gesture

The most striking gesture in this account is the church-worker who went to "stand guard" by Sixto. The fact that she was a woman suggests the character of Mary Magdalene and the other women standing guard by the cross of Jesus, and later at the empty tomb. Unlike police or military personnel who customarily stand guard to confine activity and control movement, the women stood guard to bear witness and spread the news of life arising from death.

The churchworker in this case reenacted the women's role by taking Sixto to a hospital where he could receive proper treatment and by spreading the word of what had happened so that justice might be done.

Image

There is a clear image in the sentence: "In pressing the case we hope to put the brakes on police violence. . . ." Putting on the brakes implies motorized means of travel; one doesn't put the brakes on a horse or mule or llama. In this case modern violence is like a runaway engine that will overrun whatever stands in its path.

To brake it, one has to get inside and regain control. This requires action within the system, "pressing the legal case," and mounting popular support to make the system work for the people. Sixto typifies what it takes, for "His courage has allowed him to be very clear in his testimony in the case."

A Visit with Elizabeth

Elizabeth (E) is an elderly member of the Church where I work. I (Minister) had never visited her before and had talked with her only once about the possibility of visiting. When I called to arrange for a visit, I sensed much hesitancy and apprehension in her voice.

As I knocked on the front door, I noticed an elderly lady who peered through the window at me, moved cautiously to the door, and unbolted several heavy locks. Walking in, I greeted her:

M1	Hello, Mrs. H. Thanks for letting me come over to visit.
E1	It is nice of you to come by, uh, Reverend?
M2	Please call me John. May I call you Elizabeth?
E2	Well, I suppose that's all right. I hope you don't mind sitting in the living room. It tends to be a little warm for most people.
M3	I don't mind at all. (Elizabeth looks like she doesn't know where to sit. Her chairs are distantly spaced from each other in the large, formal living room so I ask:) Is it ok for me to move this chair closer toward the couch?
E3	Uh, yes, that's all right.
M4	You know, Elizabeth, I have been intending to come to visit you for some time now. I'm glad we could finally find this time to talk.
E4	Well, I guess everyone keeps so busy, especially during December and January.
M5	Yes, that's true. . . . Do you live here by yourself?
E5	Yes. I've been alone since my husband died ten years ago.
M6	Do you have any children or relatives nearby?
E6	I don't have any children alive. Both of them died a long time ago. My nephew and I are very close. He visits every Sunday afternoon and calls almost every day to see how I am doing. He really watches out for me. I also have a niece who teaches at a neighborhood school. She is always coming over to see me. They are my family. I don't know what I would do without them. Of course, there are friends in the neighborhood who help me, so I really don't have any problems living here. The Lord has been very good to me, having these people to look after me.
M7	It sounds like you really appreciate these friends and relatives.
E7	Oh yes, I'm always having them over for lunch.

M8   I hope you don't always get stuck with the cooking.

E8   Oh my, no. We always work together. I really enjoy their company, and I can't let my house get dirty because I never know when they're going to stop in for a surprise visit.

M9   This is a pretty big house to keep clean. Do you do it all by yourself?

E9   Oh yes. Every day I do a little cleaning. It's not that hard.

M10   (Noticing the brass, pewter, and ceramic knicknacks throughout the living room, I remark:) It looks like you have quite a bit of work just dusting and polishing these little statues. They are really pretty. Do you collect them?

E10   Over the years. I have managed to accumulate over a hundred of those German Hummels. They are my favorite. I bet you would like to see some genuine Irish crystal. My husband and I purchased these when we travelled to Europe many years ago.
(We move to her dining room and she proudly opens her display of china, silver, and crystal. She really seems to enjoy talking about her collection and how she and her husband gradually amassed everything.)

M11   Elizabeth, thank you for letting me see your collection. You seem to be very proud of them. I bet they also have a special sentimental value.

E11   Yes, they certainly do. Whenever I pick up one of these statues, I think of my husband and our trips overseas. They hold dear memories for me. I treasure them very much.

M12   I sensed that, Elizabeth. I have some souvenirs at home which have special memories attached to them. I think I know what you mean about how these things help us think of people that we miss or places that we have shared with others.

E12   I also like to share these stories about how we got them or little incidents attached to them. They give my visitors a peek into my life.

M13   Yes, I agree with you. (She begins to talk about her travels, her job, her marriage. After about an hour, I get up to leave.)

E13   John, I'm so glad you could stop by. Please feel free to stop by anytime when you're in the neighborhood. Maybe you could come over sometime when my nephew is visiting. I'd like for you to meet him.

M14   Thank you, Elizabeth. I have really enjoyed our visit. I look forward to meeting your nephew. I'll stop by again soon.

Commentary

In this verbatim, John reports a very ordinary visit which does not seem to have any great theological significance. Are there any clues here that might help a person enter the experience and learn its theological lessons?

Gesture

The opening of the verbatim contains a gesture which might trigger a person's theological imagination. It occurs in the description of Elizabeth letting John in. She "peers" through the window, moves "cautiously" to the door, and unbolts "several locks." These are certainly the gestures of a hesitant person, verifying John's impression from his phone call that Elizabeth was apprehensive about his visit.

These same gestures recall the description of Jesus' disciples gathered in the upper room after his death. According to John's Gospel (20:19) "the doors of the house where the disciples had met were locked for fear of the Jews." The verbatim does not indicate that Elizabeth is actually afraid, but she is certainly locked in and wary.

The Gospel goes on to say that, despite the locked doors, Jesus came and gave his peace to them. As he shared himself with them, he brought them joy. This constitutes a ministerial agenda for John's visit with Elizabeth, one which he seems eager to fulfill.

Even though their conversation was awkward at first and a little mundane throughout, it is obvious that Elizabeth began to relax and enjoy the visit. By the end she even wanted John to meet her nephew. This has a striking parallel to the Gospel story.

When Jesus first visited the disciples after his resurrection, Thomas was not present. The Gospel doesn't say that the disciples invited Jesus back, but they certainly wanted Thomas to share the experience of his visit, which he did, eventually.

Elizabeth experienced the same sort of change which the disciples did, from caution and apprehension to peace and invitation. The fact that the visit ended with Elizabeth wanting to share the experience with her nephew and broaden the circle of her visitors is a good indication that something happened worth reflecting on theologically.

Objects

The turning point in John's visit with Elizabeth came when he noticed the "knicknacks" in her living room. It was this observation that prompted her to take him to another room, to open another door, and to begin sharing with him the objects which were far more than knicknacks to her.

Elizabeth did not seem possessive of these artifacts so much as appreciative of them. They "put her in touch" with her husband and the life she had lived with him. They were beyond the value of an appraiser, for they gave form and substance to her deepest treasures.

Imagining her handling each one, passing them to John with a comment or anecdote about their meaning brings to life the saying "Do not store up for yourselves treasures on earth, where moth and rust consume and where thieves break in and steal; but store up for yourselves treasures in heaven, where neither moth nor rust consumes and where thieves do not break in and steal. For where your treasure is, there your heart will be also" (Matt 6:19-21).

Elizabeth's heart was in her life with her husband; her treasure was her memories, immune from corruption and theft. Her objects preserved this in a way that might have prompted Jesus to say, "That's what I mean."

John seemed to sense this when he observed, "I bet they also have a special sentimental value." Sentimental value is too weak an evaluation, as Elizabeth graciously corrected: "They hold dear memories for me. I treasure them very much." Nonetheless, John's instincts were right on target.

Image

This exchange leads to a striking image which Elizabeth used. Her treasured objects give visitors "a peek" into her life. It is a life she values and wants to share with others, but it is too precious to let just anyone in, to sum up on a resume, to reduce to this or that achievement.

From this perspective Elizabeth's opening gesture is even more poignant. She "peeks" out her window at this stranger and cautiously feels her way toward deciding how much of a peek she will allow him into her life. Once satisfied that he is sincere and attentive and trustworthy, she opens the door.

Great mysteries should be handled the same way. Jesus himself unfolded the mystery of God's reign gradually, in images and parables, giving his hearers as much as he felt they could grasp or appreciate. And in the end, they marvelled like John "if every one of them [the things that Jesus did] were written down, I suppose that the world itself could not contain the books that would be written" (John 21:25). That's why images and objects and gestures are such invaluable clues for theological reflection.

Practical Suggestions and Questions

The following points summarize the material in this chapter about entering an experience. The questions suggest practical criteria which can be used to evaluate how well members of theological reflection groups enter each other's experiences.

1. To discover the presence of God in an experience, you have to enter the experience on its own terms, following the clues provided by the players, the plot, and the place.

- Are you comfortable taking this indirect course or do you need to have more explicit theological categories in mind from the outset?
- Do you agree that an experience teaches only when you enter it and become part of it?

- Do you have a different way of entering an experience besides the players, the plot, and the place?

2. People use images to express what they are feeling most deeply or what they sense is really important, especially when they can't articulate it more analytically or logically.

- Do you pay attention to people's images?
- How do you help people explore the meaning of their images?
- How do you cultivate your own imagination?
- Do images put you in touch with God's Word?

3. Objects focus and concretize the flow of a person's experience, sometimes deliberately, often unconsciously.

- Do you appreciate the role of objects in people's lives?
- How do you determine the meaning of people's objects and the way they use them?
- Can you relate this meaning to the use of objects in the Christian tradition, for example, in church art and architecture, or to practices like tithing and stewardship?
- Do objects put you in touch with God's creativity?

4. Gestures are action words, expressing all at once what many words or objects would take to convey.

- Do you notice people's gestures?
- Does it make a difference whether they use gestures consciously or unconsciously? whether they are planned or spontaneous?
- Can you relate ordinary, spontaneous gestures to the ritual gestures of worship, blessing, prayer?
- Do gestures put you in touch with God's Holy Spirit?

5. Theological reflection looks for God's presence without knowing ahead of time where or how it will appear, or even what it will be.

- Do you rely mostly on your own insights when you do theological reflection or do you seek out what others think?
- Do you take seriously the clues others suggest, especially if they are clues which did not occur to you?

- Do you expect to discover something new and unanticipated when you do theological reflection?

6. In their own ways images, objects, and gestures share in the divine life and are channels for recognizing God's presence.

- Do you believe in this connection?
- How else do human experiences reveal God?
- When clues lead to theological insight, what effect does this have on you, on your theology, on your attentiveness to everyday things?

Theoretical Background

The theoretical background for entering an experience is drawn from the following concepts in process thought: (1) real internal relations, (2) the role of dominant occasions, and (3) subjective forms and eternal objects.

Real Internal Relations

As already pointed out, Whitehead's view of reality depicts an all-inclusive network of actual occasions which are constantly creating themselves through their prehensions of other occasions. Each prehension is a conformation to some degree with the feeling quality of the object prehended. For example, the minister's prehension of David consists in the way the minister feels David's experience of drawing his bicycle. The result of these prehensions is not the juxtaposing of one entity with another but the internalizing of one entity by another. David's bicycle (with its meaning) becomes the minister's bicycle (with its meaning). This is what Whitehead called real internal relations.

He used this phrase to contrast his view with the prevailing mechanistic view that considered objects as external to one another, and which exert influence on one another only from the outside. Since the internal constitution of each entity was considered to be already determined, all that remained were their external relations to each other.

For Whitehead, reality is a dynamic, open system (or continuum). Energy is constantly flowing in and out of all occasions as they create themselves. This flow of energy establishes the relations which constitute each individual occasion as well as the network as a whole. The process of becoming for all occasions is a continual entering into the completed experiences of others in order to prehend what is relevant for one's own becoming.

The activity of theological reflection follows the same process. By their reflective activity, people create internal relations with the events they reflect upon. The events, such as the story of Sixto, are completed, actual occasions which are represented in a way that allows reflectors to prehend their meaning. Through the act of prehension, which may focus on the feelings generated by the players, the plot, or the place, real internal relations are established. This means that when a reflector enters an experience, that person not only conforms to some of the feelings proper to that occasion (for example, the injustice done to Sixto) but those same feelings partially constitute the becoming of the person (the reflector now feels justice more keenly).

The actual entry into experience is not an arbitrary or indifferent decision. Each completed experience (for example, John's visit to Elizabeth) is what it is and has its own definite quality to share. This is what theological reflection seeks and the key is to identify the dominant occasion which makes the event what it is.

Dominant Occasions

The standard explanation of process reality usually concentrates on individual actual occasions. However, almost nothing in the universe is a strictly individual actual occasion. Most things are composed of several actual occasions which form a nexus or aggregate. These clusters of occasions, each member of which is an individual occasion, constitute the objects we observe in the world and the experiences we have.

When clusters of occasions share a common order or defining characteristic, they are called (in Whiteheadian terminology) a society of occasions. A society is an integrated harmony of numerous, diverse occasions. Often the society is coordinated by one of the members, the dominant occasion. The dominant occasion gives the other elements, each of which has its own actuality, a cohesiveness which results in the final occasion with its own defining characteristic. This makes possible the classification of entities according to genus and species; it also gives rise to conventional terms which describe events according to their typical (dominant) features, rather than mentioning all the variety of their detail.

To enter into the unique reality of a specific, complex event (like any of the ministerial episodes in this chapter), it is important to grasp the dominant occasion which makes that event what it is. This is not always self-evident but it is always present. In fact there may be several such occasions, each one being dominant, depending on the perspective from which the event is viewed. All of these are valid ways of understanding the event and each of them has its own contribution to make toward the full meaning of the event. Surfacing this diversity is one reason why group reflection is preferable to individual, private reflection.

For the general purposes of theological reflection the dominant occasion in every event is God's presence. More specifically theological reflection seeks to understand how God's presence unifies a particular event and gives it its defining characteristic. God's presence may not be the only way a given experience is unified or the only source of its meaning but it is always included and is the key element which theological reflection is interested in.

God's presence always appears under the conditions of the event itself; it is incarnated by the self-creative process of the event. It is not imposed from outside the event on God's terms and it is not always and everywhere the same. This would be to consider God's presence in the abstract, devoid of any association with particular events—what Whitehead called the primordial nature of God. When God's presence is considered concretely, as a dominant occasion in a complex event, it is sought within and in terms of the event. The key to doing this is to appropriate the distinctive form which the event gives to God's presence.

Subjective Forms

The subjective form is the peculiar affective quality with which an actual occasion feels the data which it takes into its becoming. Because this process is self-directed and self-creating, Whitehead called the form which each occasion gives to the data it prehends its subjective form. He used the word "subjective" in the same way to discuss the initial subjective aim of every occasion. For Whitehead actual occasions control their own processes of becoming.

As mentioned in chapter 1, God is present at the initiation of all occasions. How the occasion prehends this divine presence and weaves it into the other prehensions it makes in constituting its experience is part of the uniqueness of each event. The stamp, which the occasion puts on God's presence, marking it as an experience of God, is the subjective form of God's presence. This is what people try to discern and conform their theological reflection to when they enter an experience.

For example, the minister, reflecting on Granny Cody's experience, felt her union with the land, her care for Rollie the cat, and her leisurely pace of living. These might be considered subjective forms of human materiality, of human love, and of human life. As the minister felt these subjective forms, they also conveyed God's presence in Granny's experience, even though Granny never mentioned God's name, and God may not have been the dominant occasion for Granny herself. Through reflection, the minister reworked these conformal feelings into a new experience which raised new questions such as why is loving ourselves so difficult? what is my hurry?

Recognizing God's presence in this way does not falsify or vitiate Granny's experience, nor does it superimpose an artificial theological meaning upon it. It acknowledges how God's presence as a dominant occasion gives unity and meaning to the experience of Granny precisely in terms of that experience itself. This is what it means to enter an experience and let the ministry teach.

4

That Reminds Me:

Theological Reflection as Illustration

John was presenting a case for the first time in a theological reflection group. He had chosen an incident from his summer internship as a campus minister. The specific issue concerned John's irritation with one member of the staff who frequently agreed to carry out certain tasks, then failed to do so or did not do so on time.

From his previous experience in CPE supervision, John knew how to describe the situation, give sufficient information, honestly portray his own feelings and say how he tried to confront his co-minister.

When he began the theological reflection portion of his case, John acknowledged that he hadn't done this before. He then proceeded to lay out a rather abstract treatment of the concept of honesty, the value of trust, and how important these are in human relationships and team ministry.

The effect on the group was deadening and John was becoming visibly uncomfortable when the supervisor interjected: "John, does your experience with this minister remind you of anything similar in Scripture?"

John thought for a moment, then answered. "Isn't there a parable about two workers and one said he would work but didn't and the other said he wouldn't but did?" John's groping response helped to relax the group.

"That sounds vaguely familiar," the supervisor commented. "Does anyone remember that parable?" One member of the group thought it was about two sons whose father asked them to work in his fields.

"Does anyone know where that parable may be found?" the supervisor asked. No one was sure, so the supervisor handed the group a Bible and gave them a few minutes to find the passage. The person who located it then read it. "Does that sound like your situation, John?" the supervisor asked. John began to draw parallels and the group joined in, noting similarities and dissimilarities.

By asking the simple question, "Does this experience remind you of anything similar in Scripture?," the supervisor had guided John back to his experience and facilitated the most common way the ministry teaches theology—by illustration. As noted in chapter 1, every experience illustrates some theological meaning because God is present in every experience. But the illustration is not always, or even usually, clear and obvious. It requires reflection.

In order to see how a particular experience illustrates theology, a person must be able to recognize the theology being illustrated. This doesn't require a comprehensive, scholarly knowledge of theology. It only requires sufficient familiarity. What is sufficient familiarity? A good example is John's response to the supervisor's question, "Does your experience remind you of anything in Scripture?" John had a vague recollection of a parable. This was part of his general knowledge of the Bible acquired over several years through hearing biblical stories read and preached at worship, group study of the Bible, and personal prayer.

John's recollection of this particular parable was not very precise, but it was sufficient to initiate the reflection. Then others supplied additional information until the story was read to the reflection group, refreshing their memories and enabling them to make connections with John's situation. In one sense they learned what they already knew. In another sense they helped each other learn more than they were aware of at that moment. They combined prior familiarity with a group contribution.

The Reflector's Familiarity

No one reflects on an experience empty-headed. By the time a person is capable of reflecting theologically (especially if preparing for ministry), that person has already accumulated a store of experiences, impressions, feelings, intuitions, thoughts, learnings, questions, doubts, insights, and convictions. Much of this is rightly called prereflexive or prethematic, meaning that it isn't always explicit and hasn't been analyzed or critically thought out and put into coherent order. But it's already there.

When a particular experience taps into this reservoir, it stirs up certain bits of information or prior reflection and starts a current moving that may bring along a lot of other forgotten or half-remembered items. This process is enhanced when it is done with a group.

The Group's Contribution

Because different people have different perspectives and degrees of information, the same experience can illustrate more than one theological point. When this happens, the experience teaches more completely, illustrating what is known and shared in the group.

As members of a reflection group describe what the experience illustrates for them, the learning is broadened and increased. The contributions of each member add to the familiarity of the others and enrich the possibilities for illustration in the future. To see in more detail what this means and how it works, consider the following case.

Jody's Dilemma: A Case Study

Background

City General Hospital is a full-service, public-funded health care facility serving mostly poor and low income patients in an economically depressed section of the city. It has been a favorite field education location for the regional seminary because its pastoral care department is accredited by the Association for Clinical Pastoral Education; it offers a wide variety of pastoral care opportunities, and it exposes students to a full range of health care services and procedures.

Description of the Experience

I (Jody) am in my third year of seminary training. I spent last summer at City General and completed my first unit of CPE. I valued the experience so much that I asked to remain there for my ministry placement this year and to continue with pastoral care certification. The Pastoral Care Department has three full-time chaplains and six interns, all of them men except for me.

Two days ago, Dr. Wright, the professor of ethics at the seminary, asked to see me and said: "You know how I run my practical ethics seminar—the group decides on a common project to put their ethical principles into action. This year's seminar group has been studying discrimination against women in the medical profession, and have decided to focus their study on City General Hospital. They're planning a press release and news conference at the hospital next week to present the research they've done and to propose changes. I know you've been working there and that's why I wanted to see you. I'm hoping you'll join us at the news conference. Being an insider, so to speak, and a woman, your presence would be a real support. Can we count on you?"

Analysis

I feel caught. In talking with the women at the hospital, I have become aware of the discrimination they face—lower pay than men for the same work, lack of respect for their opinions as professionals, and insensitivity to their home and family needs.

On the other hand, I've always been treated with respect and fairness by the pastoral care staff. If I take part in this press conference, I think they will feel betrayed. Besides, they've been working very hard to establish their own professional standing within the hospital. It would be very damaging if one of their staff showed up with an outside group criticizing City General.

Then there's Dr. Wright and the seminary. I respect him a lot. He's a stronger advocate of women's equality than a lot of women I know. I don't want to be perceived in the seminary as unwilling to take a stand, but I'm not a very demonstrative person. On the other hand, if I really think women are discriminated against and I'm working in a hospital that is guilty of it, can I justify doing nothing about it?

Commentary

This experience, which is presented as a case study, follows a simple format: background information, the dilemma or issue posed by the case, and the presenter's initial analysis. Against the background of the first three chapters, what can be said about this case? It qualifies as an important experience. It raises the issues of justice and of one's personal responsibility to insure that people are treated fairly. Those who reflect on this case can easily enter it through these issues (the plot) or through any of the key players: Jody, Dr. Wright, the hospital staff, the seminary students. Likewise the case raises numerous questions about power, culture, status, economics, gender and how these factors structure the situation (the place). So far so good, but does this case teach anything theologically?

Jody feels caught by her bond with the women at the hospital, her association with the men in the pastoral care department, and her reputation in the seminary. To Jody (or someone in the reflection group) this might recall the tension Jesus faced when his way of treating women conflicted with the public practice of his own male-dominated society or when he was confronted with the choice between religious principle (for example, the Sabbath rest) and the needs of people. If, upon reflection, Jody's case proved to be an illustration of these situations in Jesus' life, they might help Jody gain insight into Jesus and model her praxis on his response in similar circumstances.

Suppose the group does examine the parallel between Jody and Jesus and recalls that, for Jesus, the reign of God was always the primary value. Jody may not know much about the theology of God's reign, so members of the group might refer her to pertinent passages in Scripture or to the various ways this theme has been understood in Protestant and Catholic theology. In this way theological reflection contributes to theological education.

For the most part, an illustration affirms the theology a person already knows. This is why a person can recognize the theology being illustrated. The person already has some degree of theological awareness and sees it being displayed in the case at hand.

For example, Jody's peers know that men and women are equal in God's eyes and that this should be put into practice as a sign of God's reign. They can recognize this general principle in Jody's case, even if they aren't sure at the outset what specific action this theology requires (i.e., what the solution to Jody's dilemma is). This is consistent with the method of theological reflection, because action should flow from reflection (as will be discussed in chapter 7).

An illustration is not a critique of a person's theology. It does not examine the foundations and validity of theological concepts, although it may surface questions that lead to a fuller understanding. For example, someone may ask what equality in God's reign means biblically or how well that meaning has been lived out historically. These are informational questions aimed at comprehension rather than criticism.

An important experience, like Jody's, is likely to suggest several illustrations of theology. A group will have to sift through the possibilities before deciding which one allows this experience to illustrate the most helpful theology in the most enlightening way. This is not necessarily the first thought because theological reflection is a process of reflecting on and learning from experience. To help move the process along, the following questions may be useful.

Guiding Questions to Aid Illustration

What theological point(s) does this experience illustrate? Suppose the group decides that the most important point which Jody's case illustrates is that faith must be put into practice. What do I already know about this theology? For example, what do I know about the biblical teaching or the historical debates about faith and good works at the time of the Reformation?

Where is this theology found? For example, in the New Testament letter of James; the writings of Protestant Reformers; contemporary ecumenical dialogues.

What does this theology mean in its own context? For example, what did the Protestant Reformers mean when they spoke of justification by faith alone? How have contemporary theologians explained this theology ecumenically?

Does this illustration suggest areas of further study? For example, Luther's theology or current ecumenical discussions.

Does this experience add anything to my understanding of theology? For example, faith and works has been traditionally discussed in terms of the individual person, but the same issue also applies to institutions and social life, as Jody's case illustrates.

Does this illustration have implications for other areas of theology? For example, an awareness of how much theology has been developed with the individual rather than society in mind.

It is not necessary to answer all these questions, although the first four are essential for adequate theological reflection. The remaining questions may be taken up at another time or in another setting.

To gain maximum benefit from an illustration, it is helpful to be aware of the various ways an experience can illustrate theology.

How Experience Illustrates Theology

In general, experience illustrates theology in three ways: as a concrete illustration of a general theme, a contemporary illustration of a historical event, or a personal illustration of a common experience.

1. *A Concrete Illustration of a General Theme*

Most often experience provides a particular and concrete example of a general, theological theme. In one sense this is a return to origins. Even though most people learn theology abstractly and thematically, all theological themes began as concrete events. When enough events of a similar type occur, theologians summarize them in a general theme; they abstract the key insight from thousands of details, thereby performing an invaluable service. Theological reflection reenacts this process by returning to concrete events and recognizing in them a new illustration of general theological themes.

For example, Shirley had heard the theme of forgiveness all her life. This was one of her first recollections of a personal faith experience, one which was so significant that it led her to study for the ministry. One day she visited a woman who had been shot and paralyzed by a bank robber. Instead of expressing (justifiable) anger, the woman said, "I hope that man gets the help he needs so he won't have to hurt people again." For Shirley this was a concrete illustration of the theme of forgiveness.

2. *A Contemporary Illustration of a Historical Event*

Sometimes experience provides a contemporary example of a historical event which may be found in the Bible, the history of the Church, the traditions of a denomination, or the biographies of outstanding individuals or communities. In this instance the contemporary experience reenacts the past and thereby illustrates what it was.

For example, Holy Redeemer Church is located in an area where there are a large number of undocumented workers with their families. Many of these people now face deportation and possible reprisal from their governments. To help them, Holy Redeemer decides to become a sanctuary church. In doing so, it reenacts a practice with roots in Scripture and precedent in history and illustrates the theological meaning of "neighborliness."

3. *A Personal Illustration of a Common Experience*

Experience also provides opportunities to make common human events personal. Events which will sooner or later affect most people during their lives remain generic and somewhat distant until they actually occur in one's own life. Then a person knows what others have experienced.

For example, Ron had written his master's thesis on the theology of death and had conducted many funerals in his church. When his father suddenly became ill and died, Ron was stunned. His grief and adjustment to his father's absence became a personal illustration of the common human experience of death which his theology described.

In each of these instances, experience illustrates the theology which a person already knows, but this does not mean the illustration is merely repetitious or without value. In fact every illustration makes a novel contribution and has a specific value.

Value of Illustrations

Value for Oneself

An illustration has value for oneself in at least three ways. First, a person becomes more convinced of his or her theology. For example, recognizing a general theme like forgiveness in the testimony of the woman who was shot enables Shirley to be more convinced that forgiveness is not just a pious ideal but a real response to life's traumas.

Second, a person becomes more conversant with theology because every illustration provides a new way to communicate one's theology. For example, after his father's death Ron is able to express his theology of death more personally and practice his grief counseling more compassionately.

Third, a person becomes more prayerful with theology. As experience and theology converge through illustration, they invite a prayerful encounter with God. For example, in addition to studying the psalms, the Suffering Servant poems, and the Good Samaritan parable for guidance, members of Holy Redeemer now pray these passages more intently as a sanctuary church.

Value for One's Theology

In addition to its impact on theology in general, as noted above, an illustration also has value for one's personal theology. When it is illustrated, one's theology becomes more complete. Every time a connection is made between the general and specific, the past and present, the common and personal, theology's meaning and implications are filled out. For example, Ron's theology is more complete now that it includes his father's death.

Second, one's theology becomes more recognizable. Illustration enables theology to become more evident in everyday, contemporary circumstances. For example, the meaning of sanctuary is more recognizable to more people because of Holy Redeemer Church.

Third, one's theology is more enduring. Illustration makes theology part of life in its ongoing development. For example, the theological meaning of forgiveness, of sanctuary, and of death become part of life as it is carried on in the experience of Shirley, Holy Redeemer Church, and Ron.

Cautions About Illustration

Illustration is the most frequent and the most natural way to let the ministry teach, but this doesn't mean it is easy or without demands. An effective illustration requires a person to enter into the experience, explore previous knowledge, check suggested or remembered sources, carefully compare the experience with theology, and submit the illustration to the assessment of others. To increase the likelihood of genuine learning from illustrations, it is helpful to remember the following cautions.

1. Don't force an experience to illustrate a theological point and don't distort theology to fit an experience. Everything does not have to fit together perfectly for an illustration to occur. For example, in order for the opening scenario in this chapter to illustrate the Gospel parable of the father and his two sons, it is not necessary for John to describe the campus ministry staff as a family or the head of the staff as a parental figure.

2. Don't fabricate illustrations. Discover what is actually happening and let experience suggest its own proper illustrations. Theological reflection is not the same as the pedagogical task of finding examples to communicate a point effectively. For example, Ron may have wanted his reaction to his father's death to illustrate perfectly the theology he had studied and used in his pastoral practice, whereas his actual grief, feeling of loss, and moments of doubt illustrated a theology with fewer answers than he would have liked.

3. Don't stop with the first illustration that comes to mind. The first illustration may be the result of a person's most recent reading or most comfortable association rather than reflection on the experience itself. For example, when Holy Redeemer first considered becoming a sanctuary church, they saw themselves illustrating Jesus' compassion and kindness toward the oppressed which was congenial to their middle-class self-image. As they entered their experience and reflected on it more fully, they saw it as an illustration of justice which obliged them to take risks in helping the oppressed.

4. Don't stop at illustration; let the experience teach in as many ways as possible, such as application and interpretation to be discussed in chapters 5 and 6. For example, John's campus ministry experience not only illustrates the parable of the father and two sons; it also calls for an application of this parable to his future interactions with staff members. If carried out, these interactions may enable John to give the parable a new interpretation describing how the two sons might have related differently based on John's new experience with the campus ministry staff.

To see in more detail how the ministry can teach by illustration, consider the following examples.

A Critical Incident with Mr. Gomez

Background

Mr. Gomez is a very old man. He is Filipino with no family in the United States. He is partly senile and is staying at the hospital because no home for the elderly will take him. Mr. Gomez seems to be getting worse all the time. He used to sit up and talk to me, but now he lies down and talks very softly and slowly.

I didn't make any special preparation for this visit because I always stop by and see him. He is dressed only in a surgical gown, which impresses me as very undignified. He just lies on the bed, staring off into space. I sit down next to him on a chair and take his hand.

(M = Minister; G = Gomez)

M1	Hello, Mr. Gomez.
G1	Hello (very feeble voice)
M2	How are you doing today?
G2	Oh, not very good.
M3	Why? What's the matter?
G3	I don't know.
M4	Are you sick?
G4	No, but sometimes I feel very sick.
M5	I'm very sorry to hear that.
G5	Yes, so am I.
M6	Has your social worker been by to see you?
G6	No, he doesn't come around anymore.
M7	You know, the reason you've been here so long is that the rest homes in this area are all filled. That's what your social worker has been working on.
G7	(No response)
M8	What do you do during the day?
G8	Nothing. (At this, I felt sorry for him.)
M9	Can you get up at all?
G9	I can't walk anymore but I can sit up sometimes. I get a very bad headache when I sit up though. (Mr. Gomez begins to get up and it is obviously a great strain. I reach out to help him up. He stares blankly ahead and seems to face away for a minute or so, then he becomes empty and stiff. I begin to fear that he is dying right in front of me.)
M10	Mr. Gomez, are you all right?
G10	I don't feel good (very softly).
M11	Maybe you shouldn't try that again.
G11	I want to stand up. I want to sit in the chair.
M12	OK, but let me help you. (After Mr. Gomez gets settled), I hope you're feeling better now. Do you like sitting here?
G12	Yes, I like it fine. Thanks for stopping by, and please pray for me.

Personal Reflection

I guess my basic feeling was frustration. I felt like I was just probing in the dark. I have seen Mr. Gomez many times and it always seems the same. He just wastes away quietly and I come and talk. Perhaps that is all I can do and ought to do, just visit. He has no other visitors. His plight seems so sad to me, so tragic. I often wonder how he can stand it.

I was also very fearful of the scene where I thought he was dying. I could only think at the time, What can I do? What can I be at this important moment for Mr. Gomez? I was scared, I have never seen anyone die. I held on to Mr. Gomez, making me feel better; I hope it made him feel better too.

Theological Reflection

The theological theme seems to be the question of who cares when all seems to be lost. I am reminded of the story of Job; however, Job at least had some friends to talk to. Mr. Gomez has no one really. Except he has God, and he does pray. I think that would be a good topic to follow up on. Mr. Gomez, alone and in pain, with no one but the nurses and me.

In a sense I think we are all alone when it comes down to the heart of the matter. We must stand alone with our life and our decisions and no one can take our place in that. But others can be with us, and *the* Other is the most important. It is hard to see God in the situation of someone like Mr. Gomez. Perhaps I am looking too hard though. Perhaps God is right there all along, and he only asks me to recognize his presence in the very visit that I have with Mr. Gomez.

Commentary

Background

The description of Mr. Gomez is very sensitive and conveys the sadness of his present condition: he has no family; no one comes to visit him (G6); he has no permanent home (M7); he does nothing during the day (G8); he can't walk anymore (G9).

Where's the Theology?

According to chapter 1, theology may occur as a word from God, about God, or to God. In this case theology appears primarily as a Word-about-God, expressed in the minister's comment: "It is hard to see God in the situation of someone like Mr. Gomez. Perhaps I am looking too hard though. Perhaps God has been right there all along. . . ."

The minister seems to be confessing belief in God's presence while questioning that belief in the case of Mr. Gomez. If this is where the theology is in this incident, it holds implications for the role of the minister through whom God accompanies Mr. Gomez now at the end of his life. This role in turn can become a Word-to-God, which the minister senses by admitting that God "only asks me to recognize his presence in the very visit that I have with Mr. Gomez."

Entering the Experience

According to chapter 3, a person should enter another's experience alert to the images, objects, and gestures that convey theological meaning. In this case, all three appear.

In the personal reflection the minister says, "I felt like I was just probing in the dark." This is an apt image, not only for the minister's personal feelings but also for the experience of Mr. Gomez. He too seems to be probing without much success for a way to rise up and meet his God at the end of his life. There is deep theological significance in this image.

The object which stands out in the description is the surgical gown which Mr. Gomez wears. It intensifies his present undignified condition but contrasts theologically with the "new garment" of life bestowed in baptism and perfected in the risen life.

The most poignant gesture in this incident is Mr. Gomez' struggle to sit up. Theologically it suggests the "rising up" of the holy ones to meet the Lord. In this case it implicates the minister who reaches out to help and also reveals the minister's fear of death (G9). If these themes are tied in to the minister's sense that God is accompanying Mr. Gomez through the minister's visits, a rich theological reflection would result.

Illustration

The minister uses a revealing phrase to introduce the theological reflection—"I am reminded of . . ."—This ordinarily signals an illustration. In this case the general theme, "who cares when all is lost," is personalized by Mr. Gomez, "alone and in pain." For the minister this experience illustrates the story of Job. How familiar is the minister with this story?

The main parallel the minister draws is that Job, like Mr. Gomez, has lost everything, including his desire to make sense of his condition or even go on living. The minister immediately notes a dissimilarity as well: "at least Job had some friends to talk to."

This dissimilarity raises a question about the minister's familiarity with the story of Job. Were the three counselors really friends to whom Job could talk? They certainly came to offer "sympathy and comfort" (Job 2:11) but their dialogues with Job are more like inquisitions guided by the dominant theme of innocent suffering. Moreover, God was not very pleased with their pastoral care, declaring "You have not spoken rightly concerning me" (Job 42:7).

On the other hand, this dissimilarity may point toward the most helpful illustration. If the minister's visits with Mr. Gomez are seen as an illustration of the three counselors' visits with Job, what could the minister learn from those friends? What would the minister want to change or keep the same? Can the minister learn anything about God's presence from that story?

The visit with Mr. Gomez is a contemporary illustration of a past (historical?) event—the story of Job. In that context Mr. Gomez illustrates the aloneness and suffering of a good person like Job, with the hope that his story will turn out like Job's. Similarly, the minister illustrates the intent of the three friends to offer support and counseling, with implications for how (not) to conduct a pastoral visit.

If reflection on the story of Job were developed more fully, it could give the minister greater conviction about the presence of God in pastoral visits to the dying (and perhaps less fear at the prospect of another's death). At the same time the minister's understanding of the book of Job would be more complete and perhaps more useful in future visits with Mr. Gomez.

A Verbatim with Mary

Background

I am working at an ecumenical senior citizen facility that provides residential care. Most of the women and men who come to the facility are black, poor, and lonely. I have noticed that one of the women, Mary, always sits by herself and never is among a group conversing. She constantly chews gum and smokes cigarettes, wears the same pair of slacks and same sweater, and always has a knit hat on her head.

Mary grew up as a servant working for white people. She says slavery was good: "I liked it then because I knew exactly what to do." She talks about how much she learned from being a maid and how wonderful the white people were to her, even getting her a job with the government. When she became sick (she hasn't said what really happened), she had to go to a mental hospital where she stayed for eighteen years.

Each week I lead a Scripture session. Mary has never said anything during the session; there are some very strong and articulate folks and it is a little difficult to get the floor. However, after the last session, she asked me privately, "Where do you all get that faith you keep talking about?" I decided to follow this up and asked if I could visit her in her room.

(M = Minister; MA = Mary)

M1   I was surprised when you asked about my faith because you seem to have a lot of faith.

MA1   I have to be a believer because the good Lord has always taken care of me.

M2   Just like you take care of others. I noticed how you look after Edith.

MA2   Edith and I used to be roommates. Now she has to have someone do everything for her.

M3   You must be worried about her.

MA3   Sure I worry about her. It's so sad to watch a grown
        woman become senile. She used to work for the gov-
        ernment and be very active. She had strong legs.

M4   Does being with Edith and helping her make you
        afraid that someday you'll be like her?

MA4   Sure it does, but I just count my blessings. I worked
        for the nicest lady. I was a servant but she didn't treat
        me like a servant. I got to meet famous people. I even
        met John Kennedy.

M5   This woman must really have liked you.

MA5   Oh, she was wonderful. She was a Quaker. That's not
        quite as good as an Episcopalian.

M6   Why do you think Episcopalian is better?

MA6   Because they have the best food.

M7   Do you think it makes a difference to God what reli-
        gion you are?

MA7   Sure it does. I only go to church every so often now. I
        use my coffee money to put in the collection plate.

M8   You sound like you'd like to go to church more often.

MA8   I would. I need to. A woman came into this place a few
        months ago and she was blind. She came right over to
        the table where I was sitting. I didn't want to be
        around her. I got up and left. And I know it wasn't the
        Christian thing to do and God may punish me for it.

M9   I don't believe God punishes us for things that are
        hard.

MA9   I just didn't want anything to do with her. She scared
        me.

M10   Why did she scare you?

MA10   Being around her scared me that it might happen to
        me. I don't want to be blind like her.

M11   Just like being afraid of becoming senile like Edith?

MA11   Yeah.

M12   It must be very painful for you to see so much suffer-
        ing around you and wonder what's going to happen
        to you in the future.

MA12   Yeah . . . but I've done ok. I'm still able to take care of
        myself, the good Lord willing.

Theological Reflection

As I listened and responded to Mary's story, I was reminded of the person in the temple who prays, "God, be merciful to me, a sinner." (Luke 18:13) Mary will always, I think, see herself as a sinner and will seek God's mercy. Her stance toward God is that of a very humble woman who doesn't deserve very much. This attitude of humility is striking in her, yet I am also aware of the way Mary images God as a judge, as one who punishes. She also sees one religion as being better than another.

Being with Mary has been a real meditation for me on Jesus' words: blessed are the poor, for yours is the kingdom of God. I'm sure I could offer some theological comments on Jesus' words but the people at the residence live those words. Mary's story, especially of her fear of the future and possible physical sufferings, is one of being poor. Her poorness lies not only in this but also in her loneliness and her fear of becoming a burden for someone else, in becoming dependent and without control.

Her story is a strong challenge to me. I suspect I need to pray about the words of the Pharisees: "Thank God, I'm not like these others." The bottom line of Mary's story for me is, how much do I want and need to be like Mary?

Commentary

Background

The description of Mary is very factual, although some facts beg for elaboration such as her experience of slavery and eighteen years in a mental hospital. The overall impression is that of a woman with a complex and diverse history.

Where's the Theology?

In terms of the categories presented in chapter 1, the minister seems to locate theology as a Word-from-God, embodied in Mary and expressed in such comments as: "Mary has been a real meditation for me; her story is a strong challenge to me."

At the same time, Mary reveals something of God to the minister which calls for a Word-to-God, and which is summarized in the question at the end of the reflection: "How much do I want/need to be like Mary?"

Further reflection on these aspects of the experience via a Word-about-God might clarify what it is that Mary reveals to the minister and how the minister may best put it into practice, i.e., be like Mary.

Entering the Experience

In this verbatim there are no outstanding images which might give a clue to the theological meaning. However, there are two objects which Mary mentions and one gesture which is intriguing.

Speaking of Edith, Mary mentions that "she had strong legs" when she worked for the government and was very active (MA3). This strength contrasts with her present weakness and hints at Mary's concern for herself in the future, which the minister notes (M4). Strong legs sound like the kind of quality a servant might admire in another person. Knowing more about Mary's "slavery" days might shed further light on the meaning of this reference.

Likewise with the second object which Mary mentions. In recalling the woman for whom she was a servant, Mary says that Episcopalians are better than Quakers "because they have the best food" (MA6). The full meaning of this statement is not clear. The minister pursues the implied ranking of denominations (M7) rather than the food reference but the latter could easily represent the dream of a servant's life.

Mary's memory and dream are put in context by the gesture she describes in MA7. "I use my coffee money to put in the collection plate." Not only is this a sparse amount (and the opposite of rich food), it may also explain why Mary doesn't go to church more often (M8). Certainly the gesture recalls the widow who put her last penny in the Temple treasury and won Jesus' commendation.

There is something mysterious about Mary; her past is largely an untold story, but her admiration for Edith and Episcopalians gives a glimpse into her values, and her church conduct recalls biblical women who embody God's life. It is this last point which the minister sees illustrated in Mary.

Illustration

The minister begins the theological reflection with the telltale phrase, "I was reminded of . . . ." In this case Mary reminds the minister of "the person in the temple who prays, 'God, be merciful to me a sinner.'" The Scripture reference is given, Luke 18:13, and the illustration is implied in the description of Mary as a sinner, a very humble woman who sees God as a judge.

The minister does not elaborate on the biblical passage but identifies with the Pharisee while associating Mary with the tax collector. The identification with the Pharisee is consistent with the original point of the parable which was addressed to "those who believed in their own self-righteousness while holding everyone else in contempt" (Luke 18:9).

Associating Mary with the attitude of the tax collector leads the minister to recall Jesus' beatitude concerning the poor. Concretizing this saying through Mary helps the minister see poverty as including fear of the future, loneliness, and eventual dependency.

The setting of the parable is prayer and the minister keeps the reflection in this context: "Mary has been a real meditation for me; I suspect I need to pray about . . . ."

The encounter with Mary is a concrete illustration of the general themes of humility and poverty, but the focus of the reflection is on the minister, not Mary. As a result it is also a personal illustration of a common experience: how much do I want/need to be humble and poor, like Mary? How far the minister will go with this thought may depend on how honestly Mary is portrayed. There are hints of a "conditioned response" in some of Mary's comments (MA1, MA4, MA8, MA12) which could be attributed to learning how to survive as a servant. If so, this may distinguish Mary from the tax collector in the parable and call for a more nuanced imitation by the minister.

The value of this illustration seems to be that the minister is more prayerful and more conversant with a broader meaning of poverty. It could also make the minister's theology of the parable more recognizable and the values of humility and poverty more a part of the minister's ongoing life.

The illustration might be a little bit forced if Mary is not quite as humble as her words indicate. The minister may also have been vacillating between the first illustration (the parable) and the second (the beatitudes). The latter may prove more instructive theologically while the former may be more challenging personally. Both are worthy of further theological reflection.

Practical Suggestions and Questions

The following points summarize how the ministry teaches by illustration. The questions can help a person implement this material with theological reflection groups.

1. To let an experience illustrate theology, you have to be sufficiently familiar with the experience and the theology it illustrates.

- How familiar with theology do you expect students to be?
- Do you predetermine theological themes which experiences are to illustrate (e.g., ecclesiology, Christology)?
- Do you believe students may know more theology than they can recall during a group reflection?
- Does your theological reflection process help them do this?

2. Students may not recognize how their experience illustrates theology because experience does not present theology in thematic form.

- How do you help students recognize illustrations of theology in their experience?
- Do you ever ask, "What does this experience remind you of?" or "Is this experience similar to anything in your faith tradition?"
- Do you listen for illustrative expressions from a student, such as "This is an example of . . . ." or "That's the whole idea behind . . . ."?

3. Illustration is a valid and valuable form of theological reflection, even though it may not break new ground or lead to substantially new insights.

- Do you value illustration as a worthwhile outcome for theological reflection?
- Do you encourage students to look for illustrations in their experience?
- Do you alert students to the impact of illustrations on themselves or on their theology?

4. Recognizing an illustration is only the starting point. The illustration must be described, studied, analyzed, and discussed if real learning is to take place.

- How extensively do you expect a student to develop an illustration theologically?
- Is a student expected to know the illustration's original context in Scripture, history, doctrine?

5. Illustrations have effects on individuals and their theology.

- Do you ask students why a particular illustration occurred to them and what that says about their background or present stage of faith development?
- Do you have a way of assessing how convinced students are of the theology they illustrate?
- Do you help students communicate the theology they illustrate, e.g., through role plays or use of the illustration in their ministry?
- Are students encouraged to describe the effect of illustrations on their prayer life?

6. A particular experience may illustrate a theological point which is unfamiliar to the student/presenter but is known to the instructor or others in a reflection group.

- Is the reflection group used as a resource to supply additional illustrations?
- Is a student expected to take seriously the illustrations suggested by the group?
- How is this seriousness manifested (e.g., by reporting back to the group)?

7. Experience never illustrates theology perfectly; it is usually analogous, revealing both similarities and dissimilarities.

- Is a student expected to note both the similarities and dissimilarities with theology in an illustration?
- Are you comfortable with illustrations that fit theology only partially?
- What do you do with the aspects of an illustration that don't fit the experience?

8. Illustration is not the only kind of theological learning that an experience may offer.

- Is it sufficient for a student to point out illustrations or do you expect other kinds of learning (e.g., application, interpretation)?
- Are students encouraged to identify as many illustrations as possible, then focus on one?
- Is a student always expected to find at least one illustration in each experience? What if there seem to be none?

Theoretical Background

The theoretical underpinnings for the way experience illustrates theology are drawn from three key concepts in process thought: (1) God's presence in every experience, (2) the relationship of creativity and repetition, and (3) the meaning of causal efficacy.

God's Presence

As described in chapter 1, God is present in every actual occasion. God initiates each event by providing the aim which calls forth the event and God receives the final self-creation of the event (what Whitehead called its satisfaction) into God's own experience. In process theology, therefore, God's presence is always a dynamic, participating presence, and never a static, controlling presence. What more can be said about this divine presence?

God's presence endures throughout the entire process of an entity's self-creation. The initial aim which God provides remains as the goal to be satisfied through all the phases (prehensions) which constitute a given occasion. Likewise the presence of God as the recipient of the completed occasion lures that occasion to become some definite thing, to bring its experience to a conclusion. Thus, as the antecedent and consequent condition for every occasion, God's presence initiates, frames, and receives every actual occasion and can be accurately discerned only in the context of the whole event.

This means that God's presence is not simply one of the many elements which enter into the composition of an event. God's presence is not the same as the physical setting, the material objects, people, dialogue, feelings, or decisions and actions which constitute the ministerial experiences presented in this chapter. These are discrete elements prehended and interrelated in the distinct way that is this experience. These elements themselves are not God's presence; they point to God's presence. This is why they are described as clues in chapter 3 and why most experiences teach by illustrating God's presence.

In principle a complete analysis of the prehended data in a given occasion could reveal the aim for that occasion and with the aim, how God was present from the outset. In the same way a thorough knowledge of the completed occasion (what Whitehead called the superject) could reveal the value of that occasion as it enters God's experience. Of course, such complete knowledge is beyond the capacity of human beings. Nonetheless every occasion reveals something of the mysterious, accompanying presence of God. It illustrates how God was present in this event and therefore how God may have been present in past events and may be present in future events. *GOD IS IN ALL EVENTS.*

These lessons are tentative because the finished occasion may not be a very good illustration of God's presence, i.e., it may have prehended God's initial aim poorly or it may not have satisfied that aim as well as it could have. Likewise, those reflecting on the finished occasion may not be very adept at picking up its clues and reading them correctly. All of this means that theological reflection is a gradual, cumulative process. It makes small, creative advances within large, familiar patterns of repetition. This interaction needs to be examined more closely.

Creativity and Repetition

The practical goal of theological reflection is to serve the creative purposes of God. As implied in the description of God's presence in every event, God lures creation toward qualitatively new experiences. God is the author of novelty and delights in it. Of course, strictly speaking every event is a new experience because it is not simply a past experience. However, God's creativity is not satisfied with this formal, minimal degree of novelty. God seeks the qualitatively new.

The best analogy for the novelty God seeks is aesthetics, the appreciation of beauty. Aesthetics will be treated more fully in chapter 7. For the present discussion, it is sufficient to say that aesthetic enjoyment is an intensification of feeling resulting from the harmonizing of contrasts. For example, when contrasting sounds are harmonized, as in a Mozart symphony, a feeling of enjoyment is intensified. When contrasting colors are combined, as in a Michelangelo painting, aesthetic delight increases. Thus aesthetic experience requires both contrast and order. Contrast introduces novelty; order preserves continuity. Likewise novelty presupposes order and order exists for the sake of novelty.

In Whitehead's view this aesthetic pattern holds for all reality. The new emerges from the old; it is a novel configuration and reenactment of what has already occurred. And it is initiated in every instance by God who prehends everything that has occurred and envisions the real possibilities which this actual course of events now presents. The new is not, therefore, at odds with the old. It is dependent on it and derived from it. There is an unbreakable metaphysical relationship between the new and the old.

At the same time, the old has a powerful influence over the impulse toward the new because it structures the conditions from which the new is envisioned and enacted. In this sense repetition and familiarity slow down and impede creativity and novelty even at the level of human consciousness where potential for freedom and the capacity for innovation and change are so great. In fact most human beings are creatures of habit and prone to favor the familiar over the novel. This is true for theological reflection as well.

OLD & NEW ONLY EXISTS FOR HUMANS — NEVER FOR GOD.

Theological reflection, insofar as it is truly theological, should enter experience on the side of creativity and novelty because this is always God's desire. However, the new comes from the old and is only recognized as new when related to the old. This gives the past, and theological formulations from the past, a certain precedence. It also gives illustration, as a contemporary reaffirmation of the past, a certain primacy. Theological reflection in a process framework respects both claims because it realizes that the recognition of God's presence in current events cannot be achieved except in relation to the recognition of God's presence in past events. If anything, the very desire for novel experience in a process framework requires a deeper understanding of how the past brings about the present. In Whiteheadean terms this calls for an explanation of causal efficacy.

Causal Efficacy

As already noted, every new event emerges out of a network of previous events. This effective network of background influences is what Whitehead called causal efficacy. In the examples above, the visit with Mr. Gomez or the conversation with Mary were not simply creations of that one time and place and circumstance. The critical incident and the verbatim were in a real sense produced by the history of the people involved and all the other factors that came together in those occasions. Beginning with Mr. Gomez or Mary, one could trace an ever-widening linkage of previous occasions that would ultimately be coextensive with the whole world.

How much of this background is relevant in order to learn what a specific experience teaches? It is impossible to say *a priori*. This is why reflection is needed. What is easier to say is that this background is too often overlooked or disregarded altogether. In one sense this is understandable. Causal efficacy refers to the dynamic influence of factors which are not immediately evident or tangible. Human attention, following the lead of sense perception, tends to focus on striking, clear cut data.

For example, one minister observes that Mr. Gomez just lies on the bed, staring off into space; the other minister notes that

Mary never speaks during Scripture sessions. These are not isolated bits of information about Mr. Gomez and Mary; they are the product of a whole series of occasions in their lives, and to some degree they typify the meaning of that series. In turn the series of occasions constituting the lives of these two people is tied into the actual life history of numerous other people (as explained in chapter 3 under the heading of real, internal relations). This is the influence of the past which conditions every new event. The past, through causal efficacy, imposes massive conformity on the present. Novelty occurs in very small increments.

The role of causal efficacy explains why illustration is the most frequent way that experience teaches. A new experience is primarily a reflection of past events. It illustrates the larger whole which is actually (causally) connected to it and which largely brings it about (efficacy). This larger whole includes the presence of God in the sense explained above. By shedding light on the causal network behind a specific event, illustration adds one more example to the ever growing understanding of God's presence in the events of the world.

Causal efficacy also explains why a full description of every event is important and why social analysis is an important part of theological reflection. Social analysis tries to make evident the structural and sometimes intangible factors which produce a situation. A personal description can provide the sense of importance and immediacy for those who were not part of the original event, whereas social analysis describes the causal efficacy of the event and through it its larger or deeper theological meaning. Both are important if experience is to teach through illustration.

5

Now I Begin to See:

Theological Reflection as Application

Steve is a third-year seminary student. He believes strongly in the permanence of commitments, especially marriage. His parents have lived a stable, loving marriage as have his brother and sister. Though not yet married, he anticipates entering the same kind of relationship.

In his field education placement Steve is working at a residence for abused women. Recently he met Ginny, a twenty-five year-old wife and mother of two children, ages one and four. Ginny had a discolored eye and swollen jaw, the result of the latest attack by her husband who frequently leaves the family for several days without indicating where he is or when he'll return.

Ginny tells Steve that this time she's had it. After five years of physical and emotional abuse, she is prepared to file for divorce. She has even made plans to leave the state and change her name to avoid her husband. She cannot talk about her marriage without breaking down in tears.

Ginny's situation confronts Steve's ironclad conviction about the permanence of a marriage commitment. He is forced to ask: does marrying "for better or worse" include the kind of abuse Ginny has taken? What is achieved by staying in such a marriage? What is achieved by terminating it? Is this really a marriage?

The ministry provides many situations like this which challenge a person's theological understanding by calling for an application of it to a particular case. The challenge of application has been part of the Christian story from the beginning. A dramatic account of such an application is found in chapter 10 of the Acts of the Apostles. Peter is summoned to the home of Cornelius who, with his household, manifests a genuine faith and the gifts of the Holy Spirit, even though he has not yet been baptized.

Peter has to apply his still new theology of initiation to this surprising case. Allowing himself to be guided by his experience, Peter asserts, "I begin to see how true it is that God shows no partiality." He concludes by asking, rhetorically, "What can stop these people from being baptized?"

Peter learned theology in this instance by applying the knowledge he already had to a new situation. Ministerial experience often provides the same kind of opportunity. It teaches theology by presenting concrete situations in which general theological knowledge is applied. To apply theological knowledge, a person almost always has to rethink it. This doesn't mean replacing one's theology. It means looking at it from a different perspective, within the conditions of a specific situation. In this way application can lead to new insights.

For example, Steve's theology held that marriage is indissoluble. Of course, he knew that people divorced, but he attributed this to the fact that some married couples simply fail to live up to the responsibilities of marriage. However, when he met Ginny, Steve connected with her as a person; he entered her situation and identified with her experience; and he began to reassess his understanding of the theology of marriage.

Steve did not abandon his conviction that true marriage is indissoluble but he was challenged to apply his conviction to the actual circumstances of Ginny and others like her. He could no longer assume that a legal marriage was a true (indissoluble) marriage or that Ginny was a failure because she had not fulfilled his understanding of marriage. By rethinking his theology in light of Ginny's case, Steve let his ministry teach him by application.

Clarification

What Application Is Not

Application is not the same as "putting theology into practice" which a person might do, for example, by using an understanding of community to structure the working relationships on a hospital staff. This type of action is essential to theological reflection but it is more accurately called praxis or the enactment of theological reflection, which will be explained in chapter 7.

Application is not pragmatic compromise, settling for what works while trying to please everyone. For example, a pastoral care department that asserts itself with hospital patients, but never with the medical and support staff so as not to rock the boat, is compromising; it is not applying a theology of pastoral care. Likewise a field education department that does not critique theology courses for fear of alienating members of the theology faculty is sacrificing too much to keep everyone happy.

What Application Is

Application is rethinking one's theology from the perspective of a new situation. This entails the likelihood of modifying one's theology (unlike illustration which leaves theology intact, as noted in chapter 4). For example, a chaplain in an emergency room who faces the family of an innocent bystander killed by a drunken driver must rethink his theology of divine justice and providence in terms of this tragedy.

Application is adapting one's theology from its customary context of abstract thought to the novel context of a particular situation. This entails the possibility of changing one's theological priorities or emphases. For example, a chaplain in an alcohol rehabilitation center meets a patient who claims to have converted to Christ. The chaplain must give more importance than she ordinarily would to her theology of conversion in responding to this patient.

Every situation is different and calls for a fresh application of theology. The key to making an appropriate application and to learning from it is the situation itself.

When applying theology, a person doesn't impose it so much as nuance it by relating it to a particular situation. For example, in light of his experience with Ginny, Steve might be more explicit that his view is an ideal or he may qualify his position by referring to "true" marriage.

Application tests the flexibility of theology by moving it from its customary setting (academic study, reflection, discussion) to a different and perhaps unfamiliar set of circumstances. For example, application requires that the biblical and doctrinal descriptions of marriage be translated into terms that match Ginny's situation. This doesn't mean conforming theology to every circumstance or using it to rationalize every situation. It means applying theology carefully and thoughtfully, with sensitivity to the conditions of the case.

Social Analysis

Like all theological reflection, application begins with a specific event or situation. The event calls for a person to examine his or her theology from the perspective of this particular situation. To achieve optimal learning, it helps to have a systematic way of analyzing a situation. Most situations are more complex, and more instructive, than a person is initially aware of. The best help in analyzing situations is the tool of social analysis.

Social analysis can be used in any situation. For example, consider the budget of a pastoral care department, a field education program, a school, or a congregation. Social analysis helps a person see the implications of a particular budget and with this knowledge to rethink one's theology—in the case of a budget, perhaps one's theology of stewardship. Social analysis encourages us to ask a variety of questions: Who prepares the budget? How is the budget formed, what is the process? What are the criteria for deciding specific items or resolving disagreements? Who finally decides how money will be allocated? Where does the money come from? What values are expressed in the budget's allocations? Who is helped by this budget? Who is left out?

Social analysis tries to get beneath the mere facts and look at the sources and structures which produce them. It is intended to be an objective inquiry, free of its own preconceptions and biases while revealing those (including theological ones) that contribute to the way a situation is actually structured.

The conditions of a case are best revealed through the questions of social analysis, mentioned above and briefly listed in chapter 3 (analysis of the place). Using these questions, Steve might discover how gender or economic factors in society determine the meaning of marriage more than religious ideals or even the personal relationship between the spouses. Applying his theology to these conditions, Steve might reformulate it so that it addresses real problems (like Ginny's) more adequately and thereby advances the ideal of marriage more realistically.

Application presupposes more familiarity with theology and ministerial experience than illustration does. It requires a person to work with theology, not just to name it, and to rethink theology, not just to recognize it. Application can also result in a certain degree of change in a person's theology, and without a sufficient grasp of theology as a whole, this can lead to exaggerated or even erroneous conclusions. In general those in a second year of theological reflection can be expected to begin applying their theology. Whenever application occurs, the following questions may be a helpful guide.

Guiding Questions to Aid Application

Does this situation call for an application of theology? For example, the mistreatment of Ginny and her attempts to achieve a loving relationship with her husband call for an application of the theology of marriage which affirms the equality and mutual respect between husband and wife.

This theology could be found, for example, in Jesus' teaching about marriage and his attitude toward women and men, as well as in the confessional tradition of the Christian churches.

How does this theology apply to the players? What does it mean for Ginny, for her husband, for Steve? For example, Steve's theology may now acknowledge the limits implied in a commitment like marriage that involves another person.

How does this theology apply to the plot? For example, the meaning of indissolubility may not apply to Ginny's marriage because of the consistent abuse by her husband.

How does this theology apply to the place? For example, male dominance and discrimination against women in the past helped to frame laws and cultural practices that may make it all but impossible for someone like Ginny to fulfill the ideal of marriage.

How does theology affect the situation to which it is applied? For example, a theology of marriage applied to Ginny's case redefines the meaning of marriage in her regard and critiques the social attitudes and institutions which perpetuate situations like hers.

How does the application affect theology? For example, the indissolubility of marriage presupposes certain practical conditions which should be made explicit if this ideal is to have theological credibility.

Does this application touch other areas of theology? For example, by rethinking his theology of marriage, Steve may become more sensitive to discrimination against women in other areas of theology such as gender-based language and male-dominated priorities.

A person need not answer all these questions, but the first two are essential for a fruitful application of theology to any situation. The following points are also worth keeping in mind.

How Events Call for Application

Situations call for application because they provide a new perspective or require a new evaluation of a person's theology. The stimulus for this can come from any one of three sources, corresponding to the three main ingredients in an event: the players, the plot, or the place.

Players

Sometimes the people in a situation prompt application (the "who" of social analysis). People do this when they:

—*break stereotypes:* for example, a Wall Street investor urges clients to invest only in companies that are socially and environmentally sensitive. This prompts a rethinking of the theology of wealth and profit and how it may be used.

—*reverse roles:* a child with leukemia who consoles her parents and prepares them for her death causes a chaplain to apply her theology of death, grief, and pastoral care to this child's example.

—*display hidden qualities:* an illiterate worker in the housekeeping department comes up with the best plan for improving delivery of services in the hospital, challenging an administrator's theology of competence and charisms.

Plot

Sometimes the issues or values in a situation prompt application (the "what" and "how" of social analysis). This may appear in the:

—*terminology:* the director of a retreat house speaks of the "stewardship of space" and thereby enlarges the theological meaning of stewardship.

—*methodology:* a chaplain uses scientific medical studies on holistic health to redefine the role of pastoral care, inclining other pastoral carers to broaden their theology of healing.

—*outcomes:* a congregation's efforts to deepen ties among its members lead instead to greater introspection and isolation, causing them to rethink their theology of community.

Place

Sometimes the setting of a situation prompts application (the "where" of social analysis). The setting may be:

—*cultural:* a Filipino student has difficulty confronting other students in CPE because this is not done in Filipino culture. As a result the group has to adapt their theology and style of peer supervision.

—*political/sexual:* a student who admits to a gay orientation is denied approval for ordination, forcing classmates to rethink their theology of ministry.

—*social:* inmates refrain from joining a Bible class because of peer pressure and ridicule within the institution, causing the chaplain to reevaluate her theology of prison ministry.

No matter how an event may call for an application, it sets in motion a dynamic process that affects the way one does theology as well as the situations in which a person theologizes. This constitutes the theological value of application.

Value of Application

An application may affect a person's theology in at least three ways.

Reaffirm Theology

This is not simply affirming what a person already knows, as in illustration. Application *re*affirms one's theology in light of a new situation. In other words a person may end up taking basically the same position but with modifications required by the application of theology.

For example, a minister opposes abortion in all cases. She visits an unmarried teenager who is a high school dropout, has no job or marketable skills, and does not want to have the baby. In applying her convictions to this case, the minister reaffirms her opposition to abortion but modifies it with a clearer sense of responsibility to care for unwanted children.

Rearrange Theology

This refers to the priorities in one's theology and the relevance of various theological positions. Application may cause a shift in what a person considers important on a scale of theological truths or in the selection of which aspects to highlight from a particular theological teaching.

For example, a chaplain begins his hospital ministry with a clear theology of the distinctiveness and importance of his role. After a month he realizes that self-identity and distinct roles are not as important as collaboration; and within this area collaboration with medical staff is just as important as with pastoral care professionals. The experience has prompted the minister to rearrange the priorities and emphases of his theology.

Reveal New Theology

No one knows everything. New insights and understanding are always possible, especially when a person has limited ministerial experience or is faced with a new situation. In either case applying one's theology may add to what one already knows.

For example, a student is already convinced that women are discriminated against in society. In a theological reflection group, women students point out how the male experience and perspective dominate both the Bible and subsequent doctrinal formulation. The student appropriates this awareness and begins to replace a male-centered theology with a more inclusive view.

People cannot know ahead of time what impact an application will have on their theology. One indication that learning is taking place through application is when people hear themselves saying, "Now I begin to see . . . ." But learning is a two-way process. The application of theology can also affect the situation. This is not done by imposing theology from the outside but by recognizing the theological meaning of a situation from within. In this case theology's contribution to a situation can take several forms.

Spiritual

The application of theology can sometimes reveal the divine presence in a situation when it would otherwise go unnoticed. For example, applying a theology of suffering and divine providence to the emergency room may help a chaplain recognize how God is truly present in the tragedy of an innocent victim rather than assuming God is present only in healing and recovery.

Moral

The application of theology can sometimes identify moral issues which would otherwise be overlooked or avoided. For example, applying a theology of stewardship to a proposed budget may uncover (unintended) inequities and prevent decisions which would perpetuate discrimination.

Liturgical

The application of theology can sometimes create ways to ritualize the meaning of a situation and thereby deepen its impact. For example, applying a theology of conversion to the new experience of a recovering alcoholic may lead to a symbolizing of this change through autobiography, anniversary commemoration, or gifts which will make the person's sobriety more effective in the long run.

Practical

The application of theology can sometimes guide practical decisions and lead to more effective ministry. For example, applying a theology of inculturation to the Filipino student who finds it difficult to confront others may produce a more effective learning model for everyone in the CPE group.

Theological reflection is a mutual exchange between experience and theology. Application affects both. To learn theology by applying it, people must analyze a situation, enter into it, and view theology from that perspective. What they see and how they apply it is one way to let the ministry teach. To see what this means in more detail, consider the following cases.

A Case Study: How Much to Reveal?

Last week the campus ministry staff met for midsemester evaluations. All twenty-five of us were present to discuss our ministry to date. Toward the end of the meeting we set the agenda for our next session.

One minister mentioned the gay students on campus. Citing a recent statistic (he couldn't remember the source) that as many as one-third of the student body may be gay and noting the problem of the "churches' homophobic theology," he wondered if campus ministry shouldn't be doing more. Everyone agreed that we should take this issue up at our next meeting.

The prospect of this discussion is of deep concern to me. I have a "constitutional" homosexual orientation. In the upcoming discussion, how self-disclosive should I be?

At times I feel caught in a double bind: it may be inappropriate to say anything personally revelatory, yet it may be inauthentic and dishonest to remain hidden. Where does one cease to be prophetic and begin to be a cause of scandal? Will the scandal of self-disclosure cause some students to lose faith? Will the scandal of things left unspoken cause other students to feel there is no room for them in the Church? Is the decision strictly a pastoral judgment call, to be decided by weighing what is best for the campus ministry students, on the one hand, against what I am comfortable disclosing on the other? What criteria should inform such a decision?

Social Analysis

The scare of AIDS has cast a pall (quite literally) over homosexuality and has caused some to sniff a faint odor of divine retribution in the air. The issue continues to raise intense reactions of fear, confusion, disgust, avoidance, etc.

The origin of the homosexual orientation is still not understood and the complexity and uncertainty which surround it are at times almost bewildering. The visible excesses and eccentricities of some are admittedly bizarre and frightening, while the orientation of others lies undetected and unexpected; these are people who would otherwise be considered normal, decent, and healthy.

It seems to me that, for the purposes of this reflection, two assertions can be made. First, a portion of our Church is striving to live good Christian lives, even as they attempt to act responsibly with their homosexual orientation. Second, there is a pervasive homophobia in our society and in our Church which squelches dialogue and tends to perpetuate inaccurate myths and stereotypes.

Theological Reflection

I decided to bring this issue to theological reflection because I don't have a satisfying answer yet as to what is the most responsible course of action. I feel the tug of competing values: the prophetic versus prudence; authenticity versus anonymity; my limits and needs versus the need for students to be exposed to the correcting perspective of a positive role model.

I have enjoyed good relationships with the students and staff; I feel respected and appreciated by them. I would hate to see my effectiveness or acceptability evaporate because of this issue. On the other hand, I feel a commitment to speak the truth in love. I have no interest in shocking or scandalizing anyone, but I would not want to define myself according to what is comfortable and expected by others.

I look forward to ordained ministry in the Church. In my central role as preacher, I must announce the perennial truth of the gospel as it relates to the concrete circumstances of life. My primary task is to illumine and articulate the link between our real lives and world and the Word of God.

This proclamation must be more than words—it must be voiced in my very life as I live it. My life must witness to what I have preached; what I am must speak loudly. We would betray the very dynamic of our salvation if we were to move away from the messy human condition to find God in neater piety or ideals.

Is all of this just so much idealistic dreaming about what a modern preacher/minister should be? I do not think so. Rather I think the above parallels the life and ministry of Jesus. Jesus felt the need to shatter the structures of his day which hindered the movement and message of his Father. Even religious structures were not immune from his critique. Jesus criticized the dominant (religious) consciousness of his day while nurturing, nourishing and evoking an alternative consciousness which energized persons and communities with the promise of new possibility.

For many, the experience of Jesus produced the reaction of "all this is too much for us!" We domesticate the gospel and parables of Jesus so that they celebrate the secure and reinforce the status quo.

The task of the minister today still involves the need to challenge the dominant consciousness—of society and of the Church—when they distort the fullness that Jesus makes possible for us. The fact that some may be shocked by my self-disclosure perhaps should be a criterion of appropriateness.

What could my disclosure to the students provide in the way of prophetic witness? When I began my paper, I had one idea in mind: it would provide a sorely needed, positive role model in an ambiguous and frightening area. It could reinforce the idea that "outcasts" are still finding their way to the table fellowship of Jesus, and that we are not so different, strange, and weird as imagined. It could help to reveal that there is so much more that unites us than divides us.

But as I have reflected on this issue, much more unexpectedly began to be turned on its head. First, such a disclosure would call into question the role and nature of ministry in general. We speak so often of God's grace being operative in our weakness. Should I hesitate to admit my brokenness and stand as a "sign of contradiction" that God is found where there is suffering and ambiguity? Wouldn't this require a move away from hierarchical power toward interdependence and mutuality? I suspect it would.

I suspect too that such a transformed notion of leadership would allow us to be more of a healthily "confessional" church—to be a group of searchers who do not have to pretend to have as yet our lives perfectly integrated, and who do not have to be afraid of the human condition.

Enactment

To say the least, our God makes unreasonable demands on us! To be sure, the cross is not God's final word to us, but it is a bewildering vestibule to the resurrection which follows.

I remain convinced that my homosexuality is part of my bewildering vestibule. To walk away from it, to deny it, to cover it up so as to keep things neat, is to opt for a different God than the one disclosed by Jesus.

Yet I realize through this reflection process that I am not at this point ready to make a general announcement of my orientation to the staff at the upcoming session. In part this is because I am not strong enough; I don't want to risk becoming a failure as a result. And, in part, this is because I enjoy my work and know that I am a beneficial presence for the students in other ways.

Perhaps until I hear convincing statements from our Church that homosexuality is *our* issue because it is part of the body of Christ, it will be a responsible and sufficient response for me to speak in general terms in public and in personal terms only in one-on-one situations where it is helpful to do so. Perhaps, too, God will make clearer the unavoidability of self-disclosure if and when it is the divine will for me.

Commentary

Experience

Having to make a decision is the most common occasion for applying theology. In this case the campus minister feels compelled to make a decision while preferring to avoid the whole situation. That predicament happens often in the ministry, making this case applicable to many situations (a pastoral care department, a parish staff, a school faculty) besides the one described.

The minister does not give much information about the campus ministry staff or how they reacted to the assertions about the number of homosexual students and the churches' homophobic theology. "Everyone agreed," however, that the situation called for further discussion.

The focus of the incident is the minister's dilemma. In this respect the plot, rather than the players or the place, calls for application. The dilemma is presented in straightforward, either-or terms: prophecy versus scandal; loss of faith and no room in the Church; and a pure judgment call versus criteria for deciding. This suggests how much pressure the minister is feeling because the situation itself does not seem this extreme.

Social Analysis

The striking thing about this account is that the minister explicitly includes a social analysis. More accurately, the minister gives personal impressions of society's negative attitude, including the notion of "divine retribution," which is treated as part of the factual account.

The minister could have supplied more reliable data to amplify the contention that the origins of homosexuality are ambiguous and that the "excesses and eccentricities" of some homosexuals contribute to the problem of acceptance. As they stand, these observations tend to strengthen the legitimacy of society's "fear, confusion, disgust, avoidance, etc."

The two assertions at the end of this section focus the dilemma for the minister: a dichotomy between homosexuals trying to live good Christian lives and a pervasive homophobia which impedes their effort.

This attempt at social analysis is commendable but it doesn't quite succeed. There is no real analysis of the points mentioned while the points themselves merely present the dilemma in terms of the minister's perception of society.

Application of Theology

The minister begins the theological reflection by restating the dilemma described in the social analysis section. The desire seems to be to adapt the ideals of prophecy and authenticity to the situation without changing the minister's good relationships and effectiveness with students. But some change is always involved in application.

Rethinking begins when the minister considers the prospect of ordained ministry, the example of Jesus, and the task of ministry today. Four applications are evident.

1. *Ordained ministry:* the ordained minister's central role of preaching links the real world with the Word of God through the life of the preacher. As it is stated, this sounds like a reaffirmation of the minister's theology, asserted in terms of a homosexual preacher. The praxis of this position is not spelled out, but it seems to point toward a disclosure of the minister's homosexual orientation.

2. *Jesus' example:* the minister senses the need for a more explicit application and connects the preceding "idealistic dreaming" to the example of Jesus. This leads to a picture of Jesus as critic and reformer, an emphasis that sounds like a rearranging of the minister's view of Jesus and a recognition that the biblical evidence has been domesticated in the course of time. Again, the implication seems to be that a similar critique and shattering of structures is the task of the minister.

3. *Ministry today:* the example of Jesus is reconnected to ministry with a corresponding reaffirmation—"The task of the minister today still involves the need to challenge dominant

consciousness." The first direct application to the case is drawn when the minister says, "The fact that some may be shocked by my self-disclosure perhaps should be a criterion of appropriateness," just the sort of criterion the minister sought when first describing the experience.

4. *Prophetic witness:* the minister begins to sense something new being revealed in terms of prophetic witness. "When I began my paper, I had one idea in mind....But as I have reflected on this issue, much more unexpectedly began to be turned on its head." This is an unusually candid acknowledgement of how a ministerial situation can teach theology by calling for application. In arriving at this point, the minister reaffirmed a theology of preaching as central to ordained ministry and inseparable from the person of the preacher. This led to a rearranged theology of Jesus, highlighting his role as critic and reformer. What does this application reveal to the minister theologically?

The minister acknowledges two points that were revealed through this application. The first concerns the role and nature of ministry. As stated, it reaffirms the Pauline conviction that God's grace is operative in human weakness. Surely the minister was aware of this theme previously but now it appears "in *my* brokenness." It has a new power because of its personal application.

Consistent with this, the minister seems to rearrange the theology of ministry somewhat by stressing the "sign of contradiction" aspect. This entails moving away from hierarchical power toward interdependence and mutuality, which can result in the beginning of a new vision of the minister's relationship to the students on campus.

The second point of revelation in this reflection concerns the nature of Church. Broken, interdependent leaders require a confessional Church made up of searchers "who do not have to pretend to have our lives perfectly integrated yet and who do not have to be afraid of the human condition." It sounds like the minister is replacing one role with another, one image of Church with its opposite. If so, this can be an unsettling prospect.

Enactment

The minister's opening comment echoes the reaction of prophets throughout the ages: "our God makes unreasonable demands on us!" This is followed by an apt image of where the reflection has brought the minister: into the vestibule of a decision.

Despite an application of theology that leans toward self-disclosure at the next staff meeting, the minister decides "I am not at this point ready to make a general announcement of my orientation." Although the minister attributes this decision to the reflection process, the reasons are the same as those stated in the presentation of the dilemma. The minister seems to sense this and introduces a new consideration: until the Church admits that homosexuality is an issue for the whole body, this minister will continue to act out a public-private dichotomy. Unless, of course, God intervenes first and usurps the decision from the minister.

This surprising conclusion points up two things. Applying theology is not the same as enacting it. Figuring out in one's head what theology requires when applied to a given situation is not the same as carrying out that action. Likewise both application and enactment are difficult to accomplish. Sometimes it is just as demanding to think through one's theology in a new situation as it is to enact that theology. Theological reflection offers no guarantees. It only provides an entry into the vestibule.

A Critical Incident: What Is Community?

Description of the Experience

This year I am working at a major hospital with a large pastoral care department. There are four full-time chaplains and sixteen CPE students.

We began the year with a three-day orientation retreat in the mountains for the twenty-member team. Through prayer, reflection, discussion, the sharing of meals, a campfire, and honest to goodness fooling around, we formed a community. I was amazed at how wonderfully the bonds of friendship began to take form. I felt a great sense of acceptance and warmth in this group.

My expectations for this year in ministry soared as I began to appreciate what a special group we were. The number of men and women was even. There were ordained ministers and lay professionals. We were from various parts of the country and we represented ten different denominations. It was a privilege to be part of this group and I thanked God for bringing me to these people.

Critical Incident

Reality began to creep into my ideal world as soon as the retreat came to an end. At our first department meeting we went through the responsibilities of each member and the team as a whole. I began to experience an overwhelming sense that there was a great deal of work to do. I wondered if we could handle it. Or, to be more precise, could I handle it?

Almost at once I experienced breakdowns in communication. The spirit of prayer was not as evident as I had experienced it on the retreat. There was not the same intensity that I had hoped would continue. I felt that I was being estranged from the group.

Of course, there have been times of quality community experience. Sharing anecdotes about our work, having lunch together occasionally after a supervisory session. But overall I have been experiencing disappointment in myself and the others on the team because we have not sustained the intensity which we established at the retreat.

These thoughts crystallized for me this last Monday. My peer reflection group met as usual at 9:00 P.M. to review the week and plan for upcoming activities. We began late which has become the usual course of events. The meeting itself was chaos. There was a great deal of miscommunication, confusion, and an uncomfortable flow of events.

This was all my perception, of course, and it is open to debate. But I had no sense of togetherness as a result of this meeting. The feeling of belonging and the sense of common purpose which I had experienced at the beginning of this ministry were not present. I looked forward to the end of the meeting so I could get on with more comfortable activities.

Theological Reflection

I know there was a great deal of idealism on my part when we left the orientation retreat. I also know that circumstances are very different. We are not living together as we were then. We are busy about our lives of school and personal relationships.

The question that rises in my mind is whether or not the ideal reached on a retreat is possible in the reality of day-to-day living? I am struggling with this question because a part of me wants the spirit of community to be alive and constantly shining brightly. At the same time I recognize that reality does not expect a constant "high" on life. Communities are like individuals in that there are good days and there are bad days. Thus the question remains: What is community?

In Acts 2:42-47 Luke describes the community of believers immediately after the experience of Pentecost. A teacher I once had said that Luke is linking the Pentecost experience with the primitive community's life style.

The verb used in Acts 2:42 is "remained faithful" or "devoted to." This verb is very often used in the context of prayer. Common prayer underlies every great event or act of the early Church. Why? Because Jesus preached persistence in prayer (Luke 11:5-8; 18:1-8). Fidelity to prayer is what grounds fidelity to tradition, which is the point of unity for the community.

The Jesus experience led to a galvanizing action, namely Pentecost, by which the *individuals* following Jesus became a *community* following Jesus to which others flocked. As reality began to enter in on this early Church, the ideal community began to be smudged. We can see this in the account of the Jews who question Peter's authority to baptize pagans (Acts 11:1-2). The conflict between Paul and the Jerusalem community over the practice of circumcision (Acts 15ff) is another witness to the not-so-perfect life of the early Christian community. There is also plenty of evidence of unrest among the early Christian communities to whom Paul writes, primarily the Corinthian Church.

The implication is that the community of faith is in a constant need for conversion. The need for continual conversion on the part of the community both as individuals and as a whole points to the reality which I have found difficult to accept. The community in which I minister is not perfect and it will not be as long as there is history.

This reflection has given me a renewed sense of commitment to the ministerial community of which I am a part. The experience I had on the orientation retreat was an indication of the real potential which the members have of creating a life-giving and life-sustaining community. The parallel with the early Christian community in Acts has enabled me to appreciate the true humanness of my experience. I see myself as a minister as one who can remind the community that we must tend to our own inner dynamics if the ministry is to be authentic.

Commentary

Description

The orientation retreat is described in such glowing, upbeat terms that it feels a little artificial right from the start. Perhaps the minister wanted to stress the contrast between this original event and the present state of affairs by depicting the retreat in an extremely positive way.

Every description reveals something about the describer. In this case the minister fixes on the bonds of friendship, acceptance, and warmth among the members as well as how quickly the group seemed to come together. These could well be personal needs which could be discussed in a supervisory session. For purposes of theological reflection they create anticipation for the inevitable "but . . . ."

Incident

"Reality began to creep into my ideal world as soon as the retreat came to end." To a theological mind this description suggests the movement of the snake in the garden of Eden, perhaps an intended parallel. It certainly expresses the opposite of what the minister experienced on the retreat.

The first sign of "reality" is the amount of work to be done. This comes as a surprise and again may reveal more about the minister than about the situation.

The second sign is a breakdown in communication, while the third is a disappearance of the spirit of prayer. All of these indicators are mentioned without detail, resulting in a vague account which entices the reader to fill in the blanks. In this respect it is not a very helpful description because it is not specific or detailed enough.

The description of the critical incident is not much more concrete, except to note that the meeting began late. The chaos, miscommunication, confusion, and uncomfortable flow of events are not spelled out, much less analyzed.

The minister seems to sense this deficiency by admitting "this was all my perception, of course, and it is open to debate." The conclusion gives the first hint of the minister's expectation for community—a feeling of belonging and common purpose which creates comfort. In contrast to this experience, the minister feels estranged and uncomfortable, a situation that calls for an application of the theology of community.

Application of Theology

As the reflection begins, reality no longer creeps in but confronts the minister who admits, "I know there was a great deal of idealism on my part when we left the orientation retreat." Reality now forces the minister to struggle with two questions: is the ideal reached on a retreat possible in the reality of day-to-day living and what is community? When a person "struggles" with a question, it often indicates that the players, the plot, or the place are calling for a new application of theology. In this case the players break the minister's preconceptions of community, drawn from the retreat experience. The meaning of community (the plot) is questioned and calls for clarification in terms of the place, the relationship between the original retreat and the current setting of the CPE ministry.

The minister goes to the familiar account of Christian community in Acts 2:42-47. If the text were used as an illustration of theology, the minister would simply point out the similarities and dissimilarities. To make an application, more is required.

The minister links the Lukan description of community with Pentecost and ties this in with prayer, thereby reaffirming theology already known.

This reaffirmation leads to a mild rearrangement of priorities in Christology, stressing the persistence in prayer which Jesus preached (supported by passages from Luke). This theme is summarized by the minister in an interpretation that has the feel of a revelation: "fidelity to prayer is what grounds fidelity to tradition, which is the point of unity for the community."

Taking this insight a step further, the minister draws the implication that "the community of faith is in a constant need for conversion." By itself this may not be a revelation but it "points to the reality which I have found difficult to accept." In other words by applying Acts 2:42-47 to the current situation, the minister sees the dynamic of conversion at work in a way not seen before. "The parallel with the early Christian community in Acts has enabled me to appreciate the true humanness of my experience."

This revelation leads to a reassessment of the original retreat experience. It was not an event to be preserved intact (as perhaps the minister wanted to do) but was itself a revelation of "the real potential which the members have of creating a life-giving and life-sustaining community."

Seeing this potential alters the minister's self-perception as a member of the community and suggests a new role for the minister, to remind the community to attend to their inner dynamics and relationships. How the minister would actually do this passes beyond learning theology by application to the enactment of theology in praxis.

Practical Suggestions and Questions

The following points summarize how the ministry teaches by application. The questions may help a person implement this material with theological reflection groups.

1. To learn theology by applying it, you have to be guided by the experience.

- Are you aware of how applications have shaped theology throughout Christian history?

- Do you understand the difference between theological reflection as illustration and as application?
- Do you expect students to apply their theology?
- Do you help them do this?

2. Application can easily be confused with enactment and strategies for putting theology into practice in specific situations.

- Are you clear about the difference between learning theology through application and practically implementing theology through praxis?
- Do you help students see and maintain this distinction?

3. Applying theology is likely to change it, at least to some degree.

- Do you anticipate change when students apply their theology?
- Do students feel free to describe the changes which a particular application suggests?
- Are students able to adapt their theology from the formal setting in which they learn it, to the existential settings in which they apply it?

4. The key to learning through application is to analyze the situation as completely as possible on its own terms.

- Do you feel there is more to a situation than a student ordinarily recognizes?
- Do you encourage students to use social analysis in describing and entering an experience?
- Are you familiar with the questions and method of social analysis?
- What other techniques do you use to help students look at their theology from the perspective of the situation?

5. A situation calls for application when the players, the plot, or the place present a challenge to the student's prior theology.

- Do you ask students to locate the new or challenging element in their experience and to reflect theologically from that vantage point?
- Do you use the experience to test the relevance of the student's theological application?

- Do you help students look at their theology from various aspects rather than focusing only on the players or the plot?
- How do you insure a balanced and reasonably complete view of the experience (and therefore of theological learning)?

6. Application helps a student learn theology by reaffirming it, rearranging it, or revealing new insights into it.

- Do you foster all three outcomes?
- Does one result occur more frequently than the others for a given student? in the reflection group as a whole?
- How do you help a student assess the limits of a single event if the student thinks it calls for a major rearrangement of theology?
- Are students expected to show that they are familiar with the sources and meaning of the theology they apply?

7. Applying theology can also change the situation which originally called for application by highlighting spiritual, moral, liturgical, or practical implications.

- Do your students see the theological contribution of their applications to the situation itself?
- Do you insure that they have entered and grasped the experience before they begin to reshape it theologically?
- Are they encouraged to carry their theological applications into practice with a plan of action?

Theoretical Background

The theoretical basis for learning theology by application relies on the following concepts in process thought: (1) the importance of perspective, (2) the function of contrast, and (3) the development of doctrine.

Perspective

Perspective is an integral part of the knowing process in Whitehead's view. However, it does not refer to the subjective attitude of the knower so much as the objective condition of the situation. Perspective is the way the whole of reality comes to expression in a particular occasion—what is included, what is excluded, and what is potentially available for future occasions as a result. As noted in chapter 1, each occasion is self-creative, prehending from its available world what it feels to be relevant in satisfying its subjective aim. Its perspective is what the world means for its becoming. To put it another way, each actual occasion reconfigures the universe in its own self-creation.

Perspective belongs to the definiteness of individual actual occasions and helps define their importance (as discussed in chapter 1). Every occasion is a value judgment on the whole of reality. It is an empirical statement about what is and what is not important for its becoming. By what it includes and what it excludes from this process, each occasion defines its perspective and the meaning of the world for itself (which, of course, does not exhaust the entire meaning of the world). Every event, in its finiteness and particularity, contains a statement about the world as a whole.

For example, the campus minister's dilemma about disclosing a homosexual orientation is a particular perspective on the world. The CPE minister's struggle with the meaning of community is another defined perspective on the world.

The intellectual quest is not for a single definitive perspective on all of reality but for an accumulation of perspectives which yield a more and more adequate account of the meaning of the world as it has actually developed. This requires an appreciation for diversity and an openness to novelty; otherwise learning becomes mere repetition and conformity to previous understanding.

In terms of theological reflection, the goal is to examine one's previous theological understanding from the perspective of a new occasion. Letting the ministry teach by application means acquiring the perspective of the event being reflected upon and learning what it says about one's theology. Both the campus minister and the CPE intern seemed willing to do this, opening their theology to the perspectives supplied by the situations they were in and learning from this new input.

Some events are more important than others. Their perspectives reveal more about the whole or more novel truths about the whole than other events. The relative importance of an event's perspective depends on which aspects of the whole it reveals. For example, the perspectives of homosexuality and community address more important aspects of human wholeness than do questions of following schedules or planning meetings.

Application means determining how much of one's theology is relevant to the situation as it actually occurred, which elements are relevant and which are not, and what might have happened if a different configuration of theological elements had been prehended. If an experience confirms one's theological understanding with virtually no variation, the learning is an illustration. If an experience causes a person to rethink, alter, or modify one's theology, the learning is an application.

Application takes place when the situation contrasts with one's previous theology in some important way, i.e., in a way that opens one's understanding to a more comprehensive view or a more accurate grasp of what theology means. In the case of the campus minister, it was the contrast between ministry and homosexuality; in the case of the CPE intern, it was the contrast between an ideal experience of community and the day-to-day experiences of community.

Contrast

The aesthetic quality of all experience is a major theme in Whitehead's system (as noted in the last chapter). Aesthetics refers to the appreciation of beauty in nature or art. It is based on a recognition of how contrasting elements are brought together in a coherent whole yielding an experience of satisfaction and delight. The aesthetic quality of any experience depends on the integration of contrasting elements. In art aesthetic quality is judged by the use of contrasts within a generic form, e.g., the use of diverse colors in painting or different tones in music. Sometimes the contrast pertains to the form itself, e.g., the movement from realism to impressionism in painting or from classic harmony to atonal dissonance in music. The ultimate judgment of success in art is that "it works."

Application in theological reflection is similar. A person senses that a particular experience is a contrast to the existing, generic theological understanding of things. For example, the campus minister senses that homosexuality contrasts with the conventional assumptions about qualifications for the ministry; the CPE intern senses that a day-to-day community contrasts with an ideal community. The experience in each case does not simply illustrate or confirm what has been previously learned. It opens a new perspective and the possibility for a new appreciation of how fact and meaning relate in this instance. The possibility of such a novel connection suggests new learning, and with it the development of theological understanding.

Development of Doctrine

It may seem strange that a philosopher of science and mathematics would discuss the development of religious doctrine, but Whitehead took up this topic in his book, *Religion In the Making*. His basic view is that a dogma is the precise enunciation of a general truth. In this sense dogma can represent any theological statement. Such enunciations have high value for both learning and living. However, their persuasiveness does not depend on their mere formulation, but on the fact that people have *a priori* awareness from experience that allows them to recognize the value and validity of a particular dogmatic or theological formulation. In short, dogma confirms faith; it does not create it.

Similarly, every dogmatic formulation expresses some important aspect of the truth but does not express the whole truth. However, the forcefulness of dogma, or traditional, unquestioned theology, can give the mistaken impression that it does exhaust the truthfulness which it expresses. In this case dogma can work against the search for the whole truth even as it affirms the truth which it knows.

Like everything else in a process worldview, dogmatic formulations are in a constant state of development. This development pertains to both the articulation and the application of general truths to particular circumstances. Development in either sense occurs in tandem with empirical experience. In its origin a dogma is a novel articulation which is fully expressive within its own context. But because the truth it expresses transcends that context, the dogma must be applied to new contexts.

In doing so, a person learns slowly and evermore completely what the original formulation entailed, i.e., what it included, what it excluded, and what it never even considered.

A practical implication of this view is that no dogmatic (or theological) utterance is immune from context. When a new context arises with its novel contrasts, previous words and concepts may no longer convey the truth they once did. Consequently when a person reflects in this new context and takes into account its novel contrasts, it will probably be necessary to reformulate one's theology in order to express the truth which that theology intends. This is the essential meaning of application and one of the prime motives for doing theological reflection.

6

Is That What You Mean?
Theological Reflection as Interpretation

"Linda, I wonder if you can help me out." Linda's friend, Chuck, the chaplain at the state correctional institution, was on the other end of the phone.

"Sure," she replied. "What can I do?"

"One of our inmates, a lifer, is dying of cancer and they've transferred him to a hospital near you. There's no way I can get to see him before next week but it sounds like he might not live that long. Could you drop by and visit him?"

"OK," Linda answered, looking at the stack of material on her desk and realizing she had never visited an inmate before. "What's his name and where is he?"

As Linda approached the inmate's room, she saw an armed police officer sitting on a chair beside the door reading a magazine. When she told him she was a minister, he eyed her suspiciously, then nodded toward the door. Linda assumed that meant permission to enter.

When she stepped into the room, she saw another police officer, a female, also armed, sitting next to the inmate's bed. Linda relaxed when she saw another woman and introduced herself. The police officer stared back at her. "Nobody said anything about visitors," she said, then added reluctantly, "Go ahead."

Linda turned to the thin, elderly man who had been watching her. She told him the prison chaplain had asked her to visit, at which the man smiled and said, weakly, "That's just like chaplain Chuck."

"Do you like him?" Linda asked, sensing his appreciation.

"Everybody likes chaplain Chuck," the man said, his eyes rolling toward the guard. "He cares about people." The guard did not pay attention to the comment.

"He gave me this Bible," the inmate said, motioning toward the stand where a small, worn Bible lay.

"Do you have a favorite passage?" Linda asked.

"Oh, yes ma'am. I have lots of favorite passages."

"Would you like me to read one of them to you?"

"That would be very comforting," the man answered. "Read Luke 23:32-34."

Linda found the passage and read: "Two others also, who were criminals, were led away to be put to death with him. When they came to the place that is called The Skull, they crucified Jesus there with the criminals, one on his right and one on his left. Then Jesus said, 'Father, forgive them; for they do not know what they are doing.'"

After a few moments of silence, Linda asked the inmate why he had chosen that passage. The man smiled peacefully. "It reminds me that my Savior was a criminal too."

The ministry teaches theology in many ways. Most often it illustrates a familiar meaning; sometimes it calls for an application to a new situation. And occasionally the ministry interprets theology; it reveals a new and challenging meaning.

The inmate did this for Linda. In his simple comment on the passage in Luke, he interpreted the death of Jesus in terms of its criminal character. Perhaps only an inmate, sentenced to life imprisonment and facing his own imminent death, would highlight this fact and formulate it as he did. It certainly has a special impact coming from a convicted criminal and it illustrates two important convictions of modern interpretation theory: no event is uninterpreted and every event has multiple meanings.

Interpretation Theory

No Event Is Uninterpreted

There is no such thing as purely objective knowledge, free of all human interpretation. Even sensory perception is an interpretation of "what's really there." Whatever an event may be in itself, its meaning is constituted by the interpretations it generates. For example, the armed guards interpreted Linda's visit even before she began speaking with the inmate. Their presence established the specific context for this act of pastoral care and thereby influenced its meaning, possibly even prompting the inmate to select the scripture passage he did.

Every Event Has Multiple Meanings

Meaning is not an arbitrary significance laid on top of what things really are in themselves. Meaning is what things are in the context of the interactions which constitute them. The interactions in a single situation generate multiple meanings. For example, Luke 23 had a certain meaning for Linda as part of her general biblical awareness but it had a different meaning for the inmate's identification with Jesus while the reading of the passage may have only aroused suspicion in the guards. All these meanings coexisted and constituted the total meaning of the event.

To recognize the way ministerial experience interprets theology, a person should be alert to the two forms it most often takes—critical questions and alternative explanations.

Critical Questions

Critical questions are questions which don't have a ready-made answer. Questions with ready-made answers are either pedagogical or rhetorical. Pedagogical questions prepare a student to receive information a teacher wants to pass on. "Why is Luke 23:32-34 significant?" Rhetorical questions draw attention to knowledge everyone possesses: "Christians should have a special sympathy for criminals. Wasn't Jesus executed as a criminal?"

Critical questions are different. They address a person's outlook, values, way of relating, and ultimately ask who a person really is. A critical question for Linda might be, why is it necessary for armed police officers to be guarding this dying inmate? Their presence speaks to Linda of a slavish adherence to policy over persons, which she resists, and an unnecessary denial of this man's dignity, which she upholds. In effect, the situation interprets Linda as much as she interprets it.

Critical questions come from experiences which don't fit a person's typical framework of interpretation, including (perhaps especially) theological interpretation. The incongruity or disharmony need not be dramatic or extreme. It can be as basic as wondering how an inmate with a life sentence can have such theological insight.

Critical questions expose the cracks and gaps in a person's interpretation of things. This can be disturbing because most people like to think they make sense of life. When they don't, it is a sign that further reflection and possibly change are needed. For example, after this visit Linda might realize that she has stereotyped criminals. This might raise the critical questions, whom else have I stereotyped and what do I have to learn from them?

Theological reflection anticipates that certain experiences will raise critical questions that are uncomfortable or upsetting. It is easy to avoid these questions by describing only the safe parts of an experience. For this reason, theological reflection encourages a full description of events as well as a reflection group who might raise critical questions more readily.

A critical question does not contain its own answer. It only signals that a better answer is needed than is now available. It is a stimulus for further reflection and study. Also critical questions don't go away. They remain to test new interpretations to see whether they make better sense and offer a more satisfying meaning.

Alternative Explanations

Sometimes an event does not raise a critical question so much as provide an alternative explanation. This is not necessarily a response to a critical question. It is another way that experience provides interpretations or meanings that a person is not already aware of.

Christian belief in Jesus' resurrection originated with an alternative explanation. At first the only explanation of the empty tomb was that his body had been removed or stolen. Then the appearances of Jesus provided an alternative explanation which not only explained the empty tomb but also completely reoriented the disciples' relationship to him and altered the rest of their lives.

It is rare that a single experience has this kind of extensive, radical impact. Most often, alternative explanations affect this or that aspect of a person's understanding. They alter and innovate little by little. However, there can be a cumulative effect. When enough alternative explanations come together to form a new pattern and give a more adequate account of experience, it is called a paradigm shift.

Paradigm Shifts

There have been many paradigm shifts in Christian history beginning with the shift from a Jewish to a Gentile mission and the shift in status from a charismatic movement to the established religion of the Holy Roman Empire. At the present time feminist theology and other forms of liberation theology are major paradigm shifts or alternative explanations of Christian theology. The enriching effect of these movements can suggest that every theological interpretation (and implicitly all theological reflection) should have this kind of thoroughgoing, revolutionary impact.

This, of course, is neither possible nor realistic. Theological reflection does not set out to establish new paradigms or replace existing theologies. It attends carefully to the meaning of events, alert to the possibility that this meaning may in fact be an alternative explanation of some point of existing theology.

For example, as Linda ponders the inmate's statement, "My Savior was a criminal too," she may sense that Jesus' criminal status is not incidental to the meaning of his death but is more central to it than she had realized. This may cause her to rethink her understanding of redemption and to see it more in socio-political terms than in personal, moral terms. Such a shift would not happen all at once and would be built on more than the inmate's observation, but Linda's visit could result in a significant alternative explanation of her theology.

Unlike illustration and application, interpretation actually changes a person's theology. It also changes the person, because one's theology is an expression of oneself. The change may not be radical but it alters to some degree a person's theological understanding, which in turn changes the person's relationship to an experience, i.e., to the players, the plot, and the place.

The model for this kind of change is dialogue. Dialogue partners are convinced of their positions through study and experience but are nonetheless willing to let new information or new perspectives or new experience alter their understanding.

For example, suppose Linda allows the criminal status of Jesus to interpret her Christology. She might rethink the meaning of the cross in terms of the modern problem of crime and society's handling of it rather than her individual moral stance before God and God's response to her. As Linda considers this point, she must ask whether this interpretation is consistent with what theology means by Jesus' death or whether perhaps it is even a more adequate explanation of what theology means.

This is the nature of dialogue, wrestling with the truth in the grasp of both experience and theology. It is also the ultimate goal of all theological reflection, but it takes the right experience, the right attitude, and the right group to achieve it. For those who have sufficient theological background and are willing to let their experience interpret their theology, the following questions may be helpful.

Guiding Questions to Aid Interpretation

Is this experience adequate for interpreting theology? For example, the players (Linda and the inmate), the plot (the meaning of Jesus' death on the cross), and the place (structured by social, legal, and medical factors) are capable of representing one facet of Jesus' death which is underemphasized in the theological tradition and therefore may contain critical questions or alternative explanations worth considering.

What is the theology this experience interprets? In the case of Linda and the inmate, it's the meaning of Jesus' death.

What is the meaning of this theology in its own context? The biblical descriptions of Jesus' death clearly indicate that it had a political and criminal aspect. Likewise the early preaching of Jesus' followers had to reckon with the objection that his condemnation as a criminal disqualified him from being the promised Messiah.

Does this experience raise critical questions about the theology of Jesus' death? For example, why has the scandal of Jesus' criminal execution ceased to be a scandal for contemporary theology?

Does theology raise critical questions about the experience? For example, is the inmate's criminality and Jesus' criminality sufficiently analogous to warrant an interpretation of one by the other?

Does this experience offer an alternative explanation of theology? For example, the experience of criminals may contain a special theological insight into Jesus' death because he was condemned to die as a criminal.

Does theology offer an alternative explanation of the experience? For example, if negative social labels (like criminal) and nonconformity to norms of social behavior (crime) were paired with their theological opposites (Savior, salvation), they might reveal rather than hide the true meaning of a person, as in the case of both the inmate and Jesus.

How does this interpretation affect other areas of theology? For example, other groups of people who are categorized as marginal in society (the poor, disabled, homosexuals) may possess potentially radical interpretations of theology which are closer to God's truth than prevailing theology is.

The first three questions are essential for interpretation along with either questions four and five, or six and seven. Interpretation is a very involved, demanding, and creative task. It can be adequately undertaken only by those with advanced theological background. Even then, the following considerations should be kept in mind.

Interpretation and Pluralism

Interpretation causes change. Whereas illustration adds examples to what a person already knows and application expands the usefulness of a person's knowledge, interpretation changes what a person knows. Things are seen from a different perspective and what is seen is really different.

Perspective

Some events invite a person to look at things from a new perspective. Theological reflection accepts the invitation and examines how things look (what they mean) from this new vantage point.

A new perspective is not just a different way of "seeing." It is also a different way of relating, of claiming reality, of experiencing things (including oneself). Linda's visit offered her a new perspective on her relationship to Jesus as a Savior. Relating to him as a condemned criminal is a different experience from relating to him as the benevolent Son of God. In light of this new perspective her relationship to the inmate and to the guards was no doubt affected as well.

A new perspective does not eliminate other perspectives or the meaning associated with them, but neither is it just one more interpretation added to others. A different perspective alters the meaning and importance of every other perspective, giving rise to the situation called pluralism.

Pluralism

Pluralism is not a variation on the same theme; it is the co-existence of several themes. Pluralism is not a different statement of the same truth; it is a new statement of a different truth. Recognizing Jesus who was crucified *as* one of the condemned people of society is different from recognizing Jesus who was crucified *for* the condemned people of society. These are not two ways of saying the same thing. The reality is different in each case, and yet the event which generates these different meanings is one and the same. This is pluralism.

As an exercise in interpretation, theological reflection is committed to surfacing all the meanings of an event. The purpose of theological reflection is not to safeguard only the accepted meanings already identified but to learn everything which a particular experience can teach.

Unity and Truth

The pluralism which results from interpretation can be disturbing. To some, pluralism seems to undermine the unity of common understanding and to admit in its place any interpretation as valid, if not acceptable. To others, pluralism appears to complicate and confuse the simple, basic truths which make life meaningful.

In one sense these concerns illustrate what interpretation is all about. From one perspective pluralism does undermine unity; from another perspective pluralism makes unity (as the harmony of differences) possible because it surfaces the differences to be harmonized. From one perspective pluralism obscures the truth; from another perspective pluralism displays the truth in its complexity and fullness. A closer look is in order.

Interpretation, Pluralism, and Unity

A single event may give rise to many meanings, depending on the perspectives from which the event is viewed. Linda was carrying out a ministry at the request of a cominister; the guards were doing their duty; the inmate was preparing for death. How are these three meanings held together in the same event?

One Among the Many: The most common approach is to select one of the perspectives and interpret the others in relation to it. For example, the guards and the inmate are interpreted from Linda's perspective. This is a one-sided unity. It may not accurately or adequately represent the meaning of the other sides. It can also arbitrarily perpetuate the dominance of a single privileged perspective, for example, the minister's perspective in a ministerial event or the male perspective in a male-female relationship.

One in Place of the Many: The most conceptual approach is to put all the meanings into an overriding, generic category. For example, Linda, the guards, and the inmate may all be united by the notion of salvation. This is a somewhat artificial unity, however, based on the inmate's interpretation of Luke 23. In fact Linda did not go to the hospital to save the inmate, the guards did not see their role in this way (except perhaps as saving society from a convicted criminal), and the inmate himself may not have been thinking of salvation so much as personal identification with Jesus.

The Many into One: The most challenging approach is to see how all the meanings combine to constitute the one event and therein achieve their unity. Linda's ministry, the inmate's criminal life, and the guards' dutiful functioning all existed independently before the visit. But they came together in a unique and unrepeatable way to constitute this event. It is the visit which unifies them. This is an intrinsic and existential unity. It honors the dynamic process of every event, although it leaves open the question of how separate events are unified into a whole.

Interpretation, Pluralism, and Truth

The quest for meaning inevitably has a subjective quality and suggests that personal meaning is more important than objective truth. This is especially troubling for those who believe in the objectively given and guaranteed truth of God's revelation.

When theological reflection engages in interpretation, it can appear to disregard the authority of revelation and the claims of orthodoxy. The question may rightly be asked, where is the concern for truth? Despite the desire for simple, clear cut, undeniable truths, truth is very elusive. In general there are three ways of understanding and seeking truth.

Correspondence: Truth is the correspondence of human ideas to objective reality. Things are what they are no matter what perspective a person takes, no matter what they mean personally. The guide to truth is objectivity; the obstacle to truth is subjectivity.

For example, the truth of Linda's encounter with the guards does not depend on her interpretation of their reactions to her, but what they actually said and did. The truth of the inmate's insight does not depend on its meaning for him as a criminal but whether his observation corresponds to what the New Testament actually says.

Consensus: Truth is the consensus of people who examine the same events. This is not simply a "majority rules" approach. It presupposes that people are genuinely trying to understand the nature of things and are keeping personal prejudices to a minimum. Under these conditions, the truth emerges not as objectively known in itself, but as subjectively shared among thoughtful people.

For example, the truth of the inmate's observation lies in the biblical consensus that Jesus was accused and convicted of breaking the law. But to say that Jesus was a criminal in more than a technical, legal sense or that he was a criminal just like this inmate would almost surely not achieve the same consensus.

Correlation: Truth is the correlation of current experience with the meaning of past experience. The truth lies neither in always conforming the present to the past, nor in always adapting the past to the present. The truth lies in the act of interpreting each by the other.

For example, the inmate was a criminal but is now a dying, apparently peaceful man. The correlation of these truths suggests that he doesn't need to be guarded any longer. Jesus died as a criminal and the inmate is dying as a criminal. The correlation suggests the inmate knows a truth about salvation that noninmates don't.

The implications of all these points for interpreting ministerial experience theologically may be seen more clearly in the following examples.

A Critical Incident about Anger

Background

If you saw Warren and Bette Sommers, both in their 80s and married for over sixty years with children, grandchildren, and great grandchildren, you would probably first think of serenity, harmony, and compatibility par excellence. Life seemed to be a peaceful and relaxing experience for them during their first few weeks of residence at the nursing home.

They had their own beautifully furnished room with a bath; they sat together for meals; they walked and talked together most of the time; they attended chapel services, meetings, and activities always together. I had the opportunity to talk with them on a number of occasions and always enjoyed their easy-going, pleasant manner of making me feel welcome.

As time went on, I sensed that the harmony and peace were slowly breaking down. They would not always walk together or talk together. Some of the senile, forgetful habits of Mr. Sommers bothered Mrs. Sommers now. When he would mumble and talk, she would nudge him; and when she would forget something or make a mistake, he would point it out and laugh and make a mockery of it. Mr. Sommers would be found talking with some of the other women and Mrs. Sommers would jealously summon him away. I noticed they gradually began sitting apart from each other at table, meetings, or even in chapel.

They did not talk as much anymore, yet they still were polite and very discreet about the whole thing. I felt they were too polite and that there was something wrong in their relationship but I was not sure what. No one else seemed to notice it or pick up any signals. Their behavior toward me and others when they were together did not change.

Critical Incident

The situation grew progressively worse until one afternoon. I was at the nurses' station when down the hall loud arguing was heard, and I knew it must be some kind of a fight. Everyone came out of their rooms to hear or find out what was going on since it was nap time in the afternoon for many.

A nurse came to me and told me that the Sommers were fighting. Mrs. Sommers had accidentally sat on and broken Mr. Sommers' spectacles and she was mad at him for leaving them on the rocking chair in the room. She asked me to come down and see what could be done to resolve this situation.

As I approached the door which was left ajar, the nurse in charge approached me and asked what was happening. I explained the best I could and the following conversation ensued.

(HN = Head Nurse; M = Minister)

HN1   Would you please go in and talk to them and perhaps try to calm them down? They are creating quite a disturbance on this hall. I know they respect you very

much and I'm sure you will handle it in a sensitive
way. So will you. . . .

M1   I really don't feel that I should go in right now to talk
with them.

HN2   Why not?

M2   Well, I think perhaps I have a different perspective on
the situation from talking to and observing the
Sommers when I come over here. They have not been
getting along very well for a while now but I don't
know what the problem is. I'm not sure they know
what the problem is, but anyway I don't think they
have talked about the whole thing very much at all. I
believe they are just starting to face up to it. They may
be arguing but at least the broken glasses got them to
talk so maybe they can work some things out. I'd like
to give them some space . . . some privacy to be alone
and to be themselves.

HN3   Are you surprised that old people who are married
can have problems and arguments in their marriage?

M3   Well, to tell you the truth, yes. I had never really given
it much thought before. Besides that, they are the only
married couple here so far and it must be a new experience living their marriage in an institutional setting.
It can be alienating and impersonal at times. They
need to ventilate some of that pent-up anger and feelings for each other.

HN4   I think you may be right. I like the way you're handling this and I trust your judgment. Let's leave them
be for a while and see what happens.

M4   I suppose it's not the first time they've had a fight in
all these years.

Situation Analysis

I found this multi-faceted situation in which my role as pastoral minister became one of mediator to be rather challenging
and delicate. I wanted to respect the Sommers and the needs
they had in their marriage. As well, I wanted to respect and respond to the professional concerns of the nurse in charge and the
health care team as a whole. I needed to preserve the integrity of

my role in this incident and respect the needs and rights of those living in that hall of the building.

I saw my role as more of mediating between priorities than between the Sommers. I see the Sommers as the priority so I made my decision on their behalf.

Theological Reflection

This incident has helped me to reflect on a basic misconception about fighting and arguing in a relationship. There is some communication going on in an argument and it can be used in an effective way to learn more about another person. In this case it was a breakdown in the working partnership of a husband and wife. An argument allows a very different view of another person.

The most important element is the people involved. Changing situations and environment can cause instability and havoc in a marriage. When changes come, people must change and reassess their values, habits, etc. Marriage in an institution can be alienating and depersonalizing at times. I find these important considerations and reflections for ministry.

Sometimes ministry can include some misconceptions about people, their faith, and how they relate to each other. Pastoral ministry must afford people the freedom to be fully human in their relationship to each other and in faith relationship to God. My faith tells me that God wishes people to grow together in relationship to God and each other in love. Any relationship based on faith and love in which both partners are not helping each other to grow is a poor and destructive relationship and does not build up faith.

I tend to view anger, hostility, and other very strong emotions as negative in the light of our faith and relationships. They can be negative and destructive if they are bottled up inside and allowed to fester. The actual feelings and the communication of such feelings can be beneficial to one's relationship and faith if done in a growthful, honest, open, and constructive way.

Jesus in his life and ministry was open and honest in expressing his emotions, which he did on many occasions. He grew angry with Peter and the other disciples on different occasions; each time it moved beyond anger to growth and deepening intimacy. He had to be deeply disappointed at the rejection handed to him by his own people; he had to feel unloved; he expressed the abandonment he felt by his Father on the cross.

Jesus was fully human, not in hiding these emotions but in expressing them fully. Married love and other types of relationship should be dedicated to this growth in intimacy with the other and with God. Arguments can sometimes contribute to this growth in intimacy.

Commentary

Background

The minister's description of Mr. and Mrs. Sommers is filled with enough details to give the impression of a very objective account. And yet it is equally full of interpretation. The terms "serenity, harmony, compatibility, peaceful, relaxing, easygoing, pleasant manner, feel welcome" all portray the Sommers from the minister's perspective. It may be an accurate description of what the minister perceived, but it is an interpretation nonetheless.

The opening paragraphs illustrate the principle that no event is uninterpreted. The minister's way of introducing the Sommers hints that there is something else going on in their relationship behind the pleasant appearances—an implicit suggestion that the minister has learned the very lesson the reader is about to learn.

Interpretation continues in the description of the shift in the Sommers' relationship. The observation that they are not walking and talking together is coupled with the interpretation that Mr. Sommers' forgetfulness and mumbling bothers Mrs. Sommers while her forgetfulness or mistakes prompt him to make a mockery of it. Worst of all, she is supposedly jealous of his conversations with other women.

Critical Incident

The minister's perspective precedes the critical incident and sets the stage for still more interpretation. The disruption in their room certainly occurred, but it is perceived in two different ways. Mr. Sommers is upset that Mrs. Sommers broke his glasses; Mrs. Sommers is upset that he left them on the chair. They're both right. Every event has multiple meanings.

The nurse's request adds to the accumulating interpretations. From her perspective the situation needs resolving and the minister is the one to do it. This may reveal the nurse's assumption (interpretation) that a minister is a pacifier, one who reconciles people and keeps situations calm.

Any of these points would serve as a viable entry for theological reflection. The minister, however, senses in this situation still another interpretation, an alternative explanation which is described and then reflected upon.

The head nurse's request puts the situation on a personal basis and adds another interpretation of the minister as one who is respected by the Sommers and handles things in a sensitive way. This is a flattering, and no doubt sincere, assessment and it could entice the minister to comply with the request. In M2, however, the minister takes a different perspective on the situation and supports it by observations drawn from the very relationship with the Sommers which the head nurse alluded to.

In the course of M2, the minister also mentions two items which could provide clues to a further theological reflection. As described in chapter 3, clues may appear as objects, images, or gestures. The broken glasses, which started the argument, are an object which may symbolize the broken parts of the Sommers' relationship now ironically available for all to see or they may symbolize a break-through in the blind spots they have been experiencing.

The minister also uses an image—giving the Sommers some space—to explain the course of action taken. Space implies freedom, room to move about, to be oneself. This is what the Sommers need, but it is also what the minister's theology needs, as the rest of the reflection shows.

In M3 the minister begins to formulate an alternative explanation of the Sommers' argument by looking at it more closely from their point of view. They are the only married couple in the home and they have to make numerous adjustments to living in an institution. The minister is formulating a situation analysis, as described in chapter 5, and this provides a fresh perspective on the whole incident.

Situation Analysis

This "multi-faceted" situation includes the perspectives of the minister, the Sommers, the nurses and health care team, and those living in the residence hall. As the nurses see it, the situation calls for mediation between the Sommers. As the minister sees it, the situation calls for mediation between priorities. And this perspective gives rise to an alternative explanation of the Sommers' argument.

Theological Reflection

From the outset of the theological reflection the minister acknowledges that a change in thinking has occurred. The argument between the Sommers helps the minister clarify a basic misconception about arguing and fighting. At least three points emerge. First, in any argument some communication goes on where previously there may have been none. Second, arguing helps people learn things about one another they may not have known previously. Third, arguing offers a very different view of a person.

The minister maintains a sensitivity to the situation the Sommers are in while taking the reflection in a theological direction. At first this is cast in the general terms of ministry and relationships. Ministry can include misconceptions; ministry must afford people the freedom to be fully human; relationships must help the partners grow.

Eventually the minister brings the reflection home and allows the experience to have a more personal impact. "*I* tend to view anger, hostility, and other very strong emotions as negative in the light of our faith and relationships." Now, however, with the Sommers' argument in view, the minister sees things differently. Anger and hostility are negative only insofar as they are kept bottled up inside.

An alternative explanation is "the actual feelings and the communication of such feelings can be beneficial." This may not be a radical revelation to anyone else, but it is a significant change for the minister. Looking at the issue from this new perspective and with the Sommers' experience still fresh, the minister can interpret Scripture a little differently.

Jesus' anger with Peter and the other disciples was part of his relationship with them, not at cross purposes with it. His strong feelings of rejection and abandonment had to be expressed strongly, precisely because he was fully human.

The culmination of this reflection is summed up in a phrase that has become overworked in pastoral training but seems appropriate in this incident: arguments can sometimes be a growing edge in relationships.

The minister did not plan to interpret the Sommers' argument with an alternative explanation. Their argument itself gave rise to the alternative which the minister recognized and learned from.

A Case of Talents or Gifts?

Background

I have been working with people who have developmental disabilities. One of my goals for this ministry is to allow myself to be open to the gifts of simplicity, intuitiveness, and spirituality of persons with developmental disabilities. I captured this in the phrase "mutual ministry," which implied I was going to get as well as give in the ministerial process.

Two weeks ago I was part of a team that conducted a weekend retreat for fourteen developmentally disabled adults ranging in age from about eighteen to forty. I had accepted somewhat easily that these people had gifts, but had I genuinely understood what gifts are, I would not have been so surprised by the impact which some of the commonplace incidents had on me.

Description

As part of the retreat, we visited the seminary chapel. As we entered the chapel, I saw one of the students who had worked with this group of developmentally disabled people last year. I remembered how much this student complained about

Michelle, describing her as a leech and a pest. Almost at once the student left (actually fled) the chapel. When Michelle saw him leave, she asked me why he had run. I said I didn't know.

A few moments later, she asked me if he was just shy. She said she had written to him since last year but her letters were never answered. As she spoke, I sensed a loyalty that could not be shaken and would even excuse the behavior of someone who neglected her when all she wanted was a simple greeting.

During the weekend, Eugene had a seizure. *Charlie* was the hero because he was present when the first seizure occurred and did all that was necessary to make Eugene safe. Charlie also hovered about with his advice. He himself has been seizure-prone and knows all about the proper medications. He stayed nearby to offer his advice and assistance when every-one else had gone to bed.

At lunch *Tina* sat with me as she often does. She is a very spiritual person who often says the most profound prayers. After a few moments of idle conversation, she asked me where my calling came from. I was touched by her interest and began telling her my story. When I finished, she said that was not what she meant. "Where did your calling come from? What's in here?" and she thumped me on the chest. I explained in a deeper way about my call and she told me that she felt the call in her too.

At the closing meal, *Eugene* decided he wanted to offer a toast. So he got the group's attention and told them what a good time he had had and was glad he came. He lifted his glass and said, "To God." Everyone followed suit. Then he said, "And to you, God's friends." And he raised his glass again.

Theological Reflection

Before I began this ministry, I shared the common attitude in the Church toward people with developmental disabilities— they can be treated best in institutions which care for them. When I began this ministry, I thought of myself as fulfilling Jesus' directive: "Whatsoever you do to the least of my brethren, you do unto me."

After a year and a half of working with Michelle, Charlie, Tina, and Eugene, I no longer think of them in these terms.

When I think of them, it is in personal terms by name, and not in categorical terms. They are all developmentally disabled and they are all unique individuals.

I have begun to realize that it is inappropriate to refer to the deaf or the blind as though they are reducible to this one characteristic. It's a difficult habit to break but having worked with these people and after seeing them as unique individuals, these characteristics have recessed into the background and have been supplanted by descriptions that focus on the gifts they represent to others—gifts of simplicity, honesty, vulnerability, openness, transparency, lovingness, intuition, propheticness, and faithfulness.

Jean Vanier, who founded l'Arche (communities for the handicapped), makes a careful distinction between talents and gifts. He sees talents as all those superficial things that we do, some better than others. He sees gifts as that which underlies the talent. It is important to discern the gifts that underlie the talents.

St. Paul says that "there are varieties of gifts, but the same Spirit; and there are varieties of service, but the same Lord; and there are varieties of working, but it is the same God who inspires them all in everyone" (1 Cor 12:4-5). We are not listening to the Spirit if we ignore the voice of anyone in the Church, including the developmentally disabled.

I realize how much I have devalued their gifts. It was as if I had lumped them all together and put them aside. But once I began to hear their distinct voices, they blended into a whole sound which for me has become the sound of the rush of wind that swept over the followers of Christ at Pentecost.

Commentary

Background

The minister's description of the ministry contains two interpretations in the first paragraph. The phrase "developmental disability" is somewhat unfamiliar and by that very fact draws attention to a new way of viewing people who might otherwise be labeled as handicapped or blind, deaf, crippled, etc. A different way of seeing people often calls for a new name. In the same way, a new name helps people see one another differently.

The second interpretation is mutual ministry. This phrase interprets the interactions that will occur, emphasizing that "I will get as well as give in the ministerial process." This is a common form of interpretation, describing the meaning of an activity by its intended effects.

The minister's introduction to the retreat sets up the reader to expect a change in the interpretation of ministry just mentioned. Equally important, the change originates in "commonplace" incidents which would have held little meaning for the minister before the new interpretation (not yet disclosed) and its new perspective on the developmentally disabled (implying a deeper change than just a new name).

Description

The abrupt departure of the student from chapel gives rise to two interpretations: the student is avoiding Michelle (an objective interpretation?); the student is shy (a subjective interpretation?). Michelle's view is not just charitable or naive. It explains her experience with the student and may point to a quality of the student overlooked by others.

Though no explicit interpretation is given, Charlie's actions toward Eugene suggest a protective, caring person who interprets Eugene's situation as calling for just the kind of response he makes.

The minister initially interprets Tina's question as an invitation to autobiography. Tina's reinterpretation not only clarifies what she originally meant, but leads the minister to a deeper self-revelation and sharing with Tina.

Eugene's toast is an interpretation of his experience. Not only did he have a good time, he relates it to God and the friends in his life. Once he expresses this, it is available to others, giving them an opportunity to express the meaning of the event by joining in Eugene's toast.

Theological Reflection

The minister honestly describes the attitude toward disabled people which has changed through this experience. It is an understandable attitude for those who do not have the same kind of disability, and it even seems compatible with an important religious imperative—to help the least of Jesus' brothers and sisters. It is not wrong; it is inadequate.

Michelle, Charlie, Tina, and Eugene have collectively raised a critical question about this attitude. They have asked if we see them as they are or if we only see them as anonymous examples of our general category? They are indeed unique individuals as evidenced by their interpretations in word and deed of commonplace events.

The minister now sees that it is inadequate to refer to them by only one characteristic, especially the one that is most noticeable to a "normal" person—their disability. They have other, more distinguishing features which the minister now sees as gifts.

The reflection on gifts leads to a distinction, thanks to Jean Vanier, between talents and gifts. Michelle, Charlie, Tina, and Eugene may lack certain talents but they are full of gifts. The critical question now becomes whether or not we can recognize their gifts. This is the self-discovery which the minister seems to have made. "I realize how much I have devalued their gifts," echoing the earlier observation, and "had I genuinely understood what gifts are, I would not have been so surprised."

Neither is it surprising that this new interpretation would suggest St. Paul's reflection on gifts. It is unlikely that Paul had developmentally disabled persons in mind but the text surely includes them now as the minister interprets it. In a similar way the meaning of Pentecost and the symbolism of the sound of the wind are reinterpreted.

These meanings are not so radical as to challenge orthodoxy but neither are they poetic indulgence. They are theological interpretations prompted by ministerial experience.

Practical Suggestions and Questions

The following points summarize how the ministry teaches by interpretation. The questions may help to implement this material with theological reflection groups.

1. To let ministerial experience interpret theology, you have to allow the experience to suggest all its possible meanings.

- Do you encourage students to look for new meanings?
- Do you exclude certain types of interpretations from theological reflection (for example, interpretations of Scripture or Church doctrine)?
- Are you comfortable with new interpretations, even if at first they appear to be erroneous?
- Are you concerned about the impact one person's interpretation may have on others in the group?

2. Modern interpretation theory maintains that there is no such thing as an uninterpreted experience and that every event has multiple meanings.

- Do you accept these two principles? Do you use them in your theological reflection?
- Are you able to show how the description of even the most ordinary event reveals the interpretation of the one describing it?
- Do you think it is possible to know what an event means in itself? Is this a goal of theological reflection?

3. Experience can interpret theology by raising critical questions which go beyond conceptual knowledge and ask about a person's theological values, orientation, and identity.

- What does the word "critical" connote to you? to your students?
- How do you know when a question is critical? what signs do you look for?
- Do you encourage students to identify and raise critical questions for themselves? for one another?
- How do you prevent students from avoiding critical questions?

4. An experience can interpret theology by providing an alternative explanation and with it a new meaning which might change a person's previous theological understanding.

- Are you aware of the alternative explanations that have appeared in Christian history?

- Do you expect alternative explanations to occur very often in theological reflection? Do you expect them to have profound effects on students when they do occur?
- How do you distinguish between a paradigm shift and a passing fad?
- Do you foster a climate of openness to change in your theological reflection groups, or are students expected to stay with what is familiar and approved?

5. An experience may reveal different meanings when it is interpreted from different perspectives.

- Do you welcome different perspectives in the makeup of your theological reflection group?
- Do you assume that different meanings are variations on the same theme, or do you allow for the differences represented by pluralism?
- Do you presume that one interpretation is right and others are either wrong or must fit into the right one?

6. A pluralism of interpretations challenges the unity of theology and the various ways of achieving it.

- Do you feel that unity is threatened by a pluralism of theological interpretations?
- Do you encourage students to find unity when they hear different interpretations of their experience?
- How do you try to achieve and maintain theological unity in relation to pluralism? Is this important for theological reflection?

7. A pluralism of interpretations, centered on the personal meaning of an event, raises a question about truth and especially the orthodox teachings of a religious tradition.

- How do you view the relationship between personal meaning and objective truth?
- Are students accountable for the truth of their interpretations? How do they demonstrate this?
- Is orthodoxy viewed as a dialogue partner in your theological reflection groups or does it stifle dialogue?
- How do you know when a theological reflection is true?

Theoretical Background

The theoretical basis for learning theology by interpretation is drawn from the following relationships in process thought: (1) subject-object, (2) meaning-truth, and (3) the one and the many.

Subject-Object

Modern Western philosophy, at least since the time of Descartes, has been characterized by a split between the subject (the knower) and object (the known). This split was not directly intended but resulted from the "turn to the subject" which Descartes took as the indisputable starting point of reliable knowledge. The methodology of this approach treated individual experience as self-contained and separate from its external world. It was not long before this new emphasis on self-consciousness gave rise to a growing uncertainty concerning the world "out there."

The subjective world became the private realm of individual experience and the objective world became the public realm of common data, to be acted upon. This view radically redefined the relationship of human beings to nature, one another, and ultimately to God.

Whitehead sought to overcome this dichotomy by insisting on the essential relatedness of subject and object. His doctrine of real internal relations, treated in chapter 3, is one example of this. A subject prehends the value of the objective world for its becoming and the objective world endures by inclusion in the becoming of subjects. It is impossible to have one without the other; each is a condition for the possibility of the other. Their relationship is mutually constituting, not incidental or external to each other.

This approach makes it impossible to treat reality as divided into two independent areas of subjective experience and objective experience (although there is a subjective and objective dimension in every experience, as described in chapter 1). The objective world is simply the accumulation of all subjective experiences already completed; the subjective world is the current activity of all concrescing subjects prehending the objective world and reconfiguring it according to their perspectives.

This understanding is crucial for the role of interpretation in theological reflection. The meaning of experience is not simply limited to its conformity to the structure of previous experience (illustration) or to the adaptation of that meaning to a new situation (application). The meaning of experience is also its novel interpretation (prehension) of the objective world, including the world of theological reality. This is what theological reflection is most interested in when it seeks learning through interpretation.

A situation interprets theology when it expresses theology in a novel way, in terms of the particular circumstances which define a given situation. Most interpretations are minor advances, confined to the peculiarities of the situation and not relevant for other occasions. Some interpretations, however, contribute to a new way of understanding reality itself, or at least some significant portion of it. In this case interpretation can have an effect well beyond the potency of the occasion which generated it. For example, the argument between Mr. and Mrs. Sommers interpreted the minister's theological understanding of anger and arguing in general; the experiences with Michelle, Charlie, Tina, and Eugene interpreted the minister's theology of gifts beyond its meaning with the developmentally disabled.

When the process of interpretation reaches a critical mass in a certain direction, it changes both the objective and subjective relationships in that realm. Consider the effects of interpretation on the practice of slavery, the treatment of women, the value of children, the dignity of persons, the possibility of afterlife, or in reference to the main examples in this chapter, attitudes toward the elderly and the developmentally disabled. No single event by itself produced a sufficient interpretation to reverse previous understanding in these areas, but an accumulation of events giving rise to compatible interpretations eventually redefined reality.

In a truly interdependent process both the subject and object change. It is not simply a question of subjects correcting their understanding of the objective world while the objective world remains intact. The objective world responds to the way it is interpreted; it passes judgment on both the meaning and truth of the interpretations assigned to it. For example, there is more space in the world of Mr. and Mrs. Sommers and there is more acceptance in the world of the developmentally disabled children as a result of the interpretations which the respective ministers made.

Meaning and Truth

Whitehead once said that it is more important that a proposition be interesting than that it be true. He did not mean that truth was unimportant. He meant that propositions which excite, open new possibilities, give a fresh perspective on the world are more meaningful than truth which merely repeats what is already known or is relevant only to a narrow band of experience.

In Whitehead's scheme propositions are not abstract concepts governed by the rules of logic. They are prereflective feelings which arise from a particular occasion and urge the inclusion of that occasion in future enactments. A proposition is an occasion's claim to relevance, signaling in effect that it has something worthwhile to contribute to the ongoing process of becoming. This appeal goes beyond the realm bounded by logic and other special sciences. It addresses the realm of creativity and novelty—the realm of highest value in a process worldview.

Interpretation is essentially discovering what is interesting in experience and following its lead, envisioning what future experience would be like if this or that interesting element were included. Truthful propositions enhance this interest factor more than false propositions and are also more likely to prompt satisfying action, but the real value of any proposition is its interest as a stimulus for becoming.

Theological reflection seeks the truth that creates, the truth that explores the not yet thought or expressed possibilities of reality. The stimulus for this search is the interest found in the propositional quality of the experiences which are reflected upon. This propositional quality is not an abstract formulation "of what the experience really means." It is a concrete appeal to what the experience might mean. In this sense one minister found the Sommers' argument an interesting proposition and the other minister found the children's gifts an interesting proposition.

Important experiences may generate numerous appeals of this type, especially if they are reflected upon by a group. This capacity raises the question of the one and the many.

The One and the Many

Whitehead's concern with this question was primarily cosmological. He was interested in the physical objects which make up the world, display a stunning variety, and yet seem to share a common metaphysical nature. The same challenge confronts epistemology. How does one reconcile the multiplicity of interpretations with the presumed unity of truth? In both instances Whitehead's response is overtly theological.

A process world is radically pluralistic, even atomistic in the sense that reality is ultimately constituted by the self-creation of individual actual occasions. These occasions are not predetermined nor can they be known *a priori*, not even by God. They are what they are by virtue of their own, unrepeatable self creation. And yet, this multiplicity (generically called the world) evidences order and unity rather than randomness and chaos. Why? Because of God.

God takes the world into the divine experience, adjusts it to God's own ideal envisagement, and generates a new vision which establishes both the unity of the existing world and the order for its next creative surge. This unity and order are fluid, interacting constantly with the actual occasions and concrescing entities which make up the world. God is steadfast in pursuit of the highest ideals (truth, beauty, goodness, freedom, peace) but the order for attaining them depends on the actual occasions which constitute the world as it is.

Theological reflection tries to do the same thing within the limited horizon of the experience it reflects upon. In essence it tries to think with God, to discern the unity God may see in a given event and the order God may suggest for the subsequent events which flow from it. Rather than interpreting the Sommers' argument as a sign of disunity, the minister senses that it can be the opening of emotions and establishing of an order that will allow them to communicate better in the future. Rather than looking for talents which are not present, the minister learns to interpret the actions of the developmentally disabled as gifts; as a result, a new unity appears which embraces both the normal and the disabled.

Theological systems, doctrines, and traditions are valuable assets in this search, but they do not take the place of interpretation. They may represent the union of the many from the past, but they may have to change to accommodate the new events being created in the present. Theological reflectors are never closer to God in a process worldview than when they seek to unify the many by letting the meaning of events guide them to the truth and open up the next possibilities for order, creativity, and becoming. This is to let the ministry teach at its best and fullest.

7

Now What Do I Do?
Enacting the Learning

Jennifer, a twenty-two year old college student, recently underwent a lung transplant operation after waiting four months for a donor. During her recuperation, three members of the pastoral care staff visited her.

When they reflected theologically on their visits, they discovered that they all referred to the image of God's breath or Spirit, no doubt suggested by the nature of the operation. Jennifer's heroic struggle to breathe normally dramatized for them the relationship between breathing and the body. This led to a consideration of Genesis 2:7 where the human body is enlivened by the breath of God. From here they considered the role of the Spirit animating the body of Jesus after the crucifixion and their own role as a channel of the Spirit building up the body of Christ by their ministry to Jennifer.

As these three ministers carried their reflections into action, they found that they were led in different directions. One of them drew personal implications. Watching Jennifer struggle for every painful breath and identifying with her spirit for life, this minister resolved to bring a new spirit of determination and commitment to the ministry.

A second minister was confronted with a change of ministerial style. Trained to be a listener and to help others express themselves, this minister found it necessary to do most of the talking because it was too painful for Jennifer to speak. Ironically this required even more intense listening in order to respond accurately to what Jennifer was feeling and desiring.

A third minister was struck by the theological implications of this encounter. The interdependence of so many people and systems coordinated for the sake of one person's health prompted this minister to reflect on the metaphor of Christ's body as an image of the whole community made up of many people with diverse skills and motives all working together for the well-being of each other.

The three chaplains who visited Jennifer were led to three different enactments of their reflection, but their different responses complemented one another because they came out of a common experience and served a common purpose—Jennifer's well-being. They illustrate three common types of enactment: personal, ministerial, and theological.

Personal Enactment

Personal enactment refers to one's identity, self-image, motivation, and feelings about oneself. Eventually these factors affect a person's actions and relationships with others, but, for the most part, personal enactment pertains to who a person is, not what a person does.

Every theological reflection entails some degree of personal enactment because reflection is a personal act, and it affects the person who does it. The ideas generated by reflection are not self-contained bits of information residing within a person's brain; they are a dynamic assembly of information flowing through the whole person affecting identity, self-image, values, motivation, feelings, perception, and desires.

A person does not usually determine ahead of time to develop theological reflection into a personal enactment. The minister in the opening scenario who was moved to enact greater dedication and commitment to the ministry probably did not have this as a goal before meeting Jennifer. The experience itself and reflection upon it with the other chaplains suggested a personal enactment as the most appropriate way for this minister to carry out what had been learned.

On the other hand, personal enactment can sometimes be the goal of theological reflection. This happens especially in the early stages of a minister's training or at times of self-assessment during the ministry or when a person begins a new ministry and is not yet comfortable in it. In such situations a minister will usually be more aware of personal identity, role fulfillment, self-image, motivation, and satisfaction. As a result, the outcome of theological reflection will tend toward personal enactment.

Personal enactment is not confined to individuals. Groups can also experience a change in their identity, image, style, values, and motives. For example, in reflecting on their encounter with Jennifer, the pastoral care staff may adopt a new collective image and describe themselves as a fresh breath of air in the body of Christ.

Theologically the most profound type of personal enactment is conversion, a reorientation of oneself to follow God's ways in daily life. An appeal to such conversion was at the heart of Jesus' message and ministry. It is surely an appropriate response to theological reflection.

The following critical incident illustrates in more detail the meaning of personal enactment.

Personal Enactment of a Critical Incident

Background

Bill is beginning his fourth year of preparation for the priesthood and is working with elderly residents at Golden Age Towers, a retirement facility. Abe, the only Jewish man in residence, has not made the adjustment well. His wife died six months ago and his two sons and their families recently moved out of state.

Bill has visited Abe a couple of times and senses that they have established a good rapport. During the last visit, Abe said he might need an operation. Bill knew Abe was concerned about this and intended to discuss it with him on the next visit.

Incident

When they met, Bill was eager to raise the issue of the operation but Abe seemed more interested in small talk.

Abe 1   You're going to be a priest, aren't you?

Bill 1   Yes, I should be ordained next summer.

Abe 2   And priests don't marry, do they?

Bill 2   (Wondering why a Jew is interested in this) No, we don't.

Abe 3   Why is that?

Bill 3   Well, it's so we can serve people more completely and dedicate ourselves to the ministry.

Abe 4   Is it hard?

Bill 4   Sure, sometimes. But I guess it's hard for all of us; even married people have to remain faithful, right? (thinking this may be what Abe is getting at)

Abe 5   Oh, I didn't mean the sexual part. I meant, is it hard to give up your own family? How do you let go of that?

Bill 5   Well, I guess you don't miss what you never had. Why do you ask?

Abe 6   Oh, I was just wondering.

Bill 6   (Ready to move on to other topics) Well, how about your tests for that operation. Any results yet?

Abe 7   Nope. Haven't heard a word.

Theological Reflection

During this visit, Bill felt a little frustrated when Abe started asking him about celibacy because he wanted to help Abe face the possibility of an operation. In fact, he interpreted the celibacy discussion as an avoidance of the real issue, not unusual for someone in Abe's circumstances. Bill's reflection group helped him to see the incident differently.

They entered this experience through the plot, which they interpreted to be Abe's sense of loss—his wife, his children, his home, his health. Then Bill walks into the room. Abe sees in him someone who also faces the loss of wife, children, and private home, but voluntarily. Perhaps Abe thinks Bill is in a position to help him deal with the losses he is experiencing.

Bill seemed to miss this connection and pressed on with his own agenda. Viewed from this angle Abe's concluding comment has an ironic application to Bill's efforts: "Haven't heard a word," as if he hasn't heard anything from Bill that would help him deal with his loss of family.

From the group's point of view this encounter was an opportunity for Bill's celibacy to interpret Abe's situation and for Abe's situation to interpret Bill's celibacy. It was also an opportunity for Bill to apply the meaning of his celibacy to Abe's situation. Some experiences can teach theology in more ways than one.

Personal Enactment

Bill's critical incident calls for a personal enactment. His visit with Abe confronted him, unexpectedly, with questions about his identity and lifestyle. Reflecting from Abe's perspective on the answers he gave in Bill 3 and 5, Bill might review his own rationale for celibacy and his degree of comfort with it. As he does, the following questions might be helpful.

How am I changed as a result of this reflection and how do I feel about myself now? For example, Bill is more aware of himself as a celibate and he realizes that the meaning (interpretation) of his celibacy can come from others as much as from himself or Church tradition.

How is this change a personal enactment of theological reflection? For example, Bill was unaware of how his identity and lifestyle (celibacy) were perceived by Abe. Now he will be more sensitive to how this may affect others and, as a result, influence his ministry with them.

Does this personal enactment have implications for other areas of theology or ministry? For example, Bill may not have previously recognized the connection between who he is and what he does. Now he is prompted to examine the relationship between "being" and "doing" in other areas of his ministry such as prayer, worship, and spiritual guidance.

Is this personal enactment a new ministerial experience which calls for theological reflection? For example, as Bill sees himself from Abe's point of view, he might reflect on the symbolic or representative role of his ministry as much as its functional aspect.

It may seem that personal enactment is a wholly "internal" activity, but changes in one's self-image and identity soon find external expression which in turn affects the way a person relates to others in speech, actions, decisions, and ministerial style.

Ministerial Enactment

Ministerial enactment refers to what a person does, how a person ministers, the skills a person develops and uses in working with individuals, groups, communities, or society at large.

Theological reflection which originates in ministerial activity seeks expression in ministry. This is seen most clearly in ministerial activity which consists of a series of events which build on one another, as in counseling, teaching, or pastoral planning. In these cases reflection on each episode shapes the course of action in the next event and the series as a whole.

Sometimes the ministry does not consist of a continuous series of events but the repetition of a specific type of activity such as preaching, pastoral care, or spiritual direction. In these cases reflection on each event is also a general preparation for the next time the minister engages in this type of activity.

Every ministerial enactment is also a theological statement which relies for its effectiveness on the exercise of skills, especially the skill of planning. Skills have theological significance when they are used to enact theological reflection. Personal motivation and theological conviction are not enough to minister effectively, nor are they enough to enact theological reflection ministerially.

Ministerial enactment is not confined to the minister—those who are ministered to play an active role. They influence both the theological reflection and the enactment of the reflection. In the opening scenario, Jennifer was an active player whose inability to converse after her operation elicited the ministerial enactment of the chaplain who had to learn to speak more while listening just as intently.

Ministerial enactment is not limited to individual ministers. The shared theological reflection on Jennifer's experience by the pastoral care staff enriched the ministerial enactment of the staff as a whole, even though each person enacted the ministry in a distinctive way.

The ministerial enactment of Jesus exemplifies these points. His ministry grew out of his deep reflection on God's will, his own experience, and the experience of those around him. He was very skillful in putting his mission into practice and the recipients of his ministry frequently influenced him. He did not keep his ministry to himself but shared it with his disciples, urging them to enact it in their own way.

The meaning of ministerial enactment may be seen more clearly in the following example.

Ministerial Enactment Through an Interview

Background

Leo and Janet are pastoral care interns at the County Alcohol and Drug Recovery Center. After a few months, they began to realize that most of the patients stayed at the Center for only four weeks, even though their addictions required longer treatment.

When they asked about this, they learned that most of the patients paid for their treatment with insurance benefits, and their insurance policies usually cover only four weeks. This situation prompted Janet and Leo to do something to help the patients after their release.

Theological Reflection

Leo and Janet presented this experience to their theological reflection group. Their entry point was the structural setting of the experience (the place), and they used social analysis to gain a more complete understanding of the situation. This led to a theological reflection on the interdependence of persons and systems, of individual needs and general policies. Janet and Leo recognized that in their theology these pairs were not equal, because they give priority to persons rather than systems, to individual needs rather than general policies.

The reflection group urged Leo and Janet to see this experi-ence as an opportunity to apply their theology (the second way ministerial experience can teach). They decided to do this by asking the patients what they needed when they were re-leased from the County Recovery Center. To get this informa-tion, they decided to interview the patients.

The interview became a ministerial enactment of their theo-logical reflection. They wanted to approach each patient in a way that would affirm the primacy of persons in their theol-ogy and they wanted their questions to express this theology as well. This is what they finally came up with.

• They would contact each person, explain the reason for the meeting, and make an appointment at a time and place of the person's choosing, thus showing respect and deference to each individual.

• They would engage in a conversation rather than a for-mal question and answer discussion, thus using a natural, friendly approach.

• They would seek opinions and suggestions which the person was capable of giving rather than asking questions that demanded specialized knowledge or training, thus treating each person fairly and drawing upon their strengths.

• They would inform the person of the results of their in-terviews, thus acknowledging the value of their time and input; and they would invite further comments on any action plans they might develop, thus enabling the clients to be par-ticipants and not just recipients.

Ministerial Enactment

Janet and Leo presented the results of their interviews to the reflection group as an illustration of their theology of the human person, using the words and feelings of the people they interviewed rather than the technical vocabulary of Christian anthropology. The group appreciated that Leo and Janet had presented an ongoing experience rather than an iso-lated event, and they reflected together on the meaning of this experience by using the following questions.

How does this theological reflection change the perfor-mance of my ministry? For example, Leo and Janet's ministry expanded beyond their work within the County Recovery Center and brought them into contact with some of the factors that structure society (insurance policies, treatment programs).

How is this change enacted ministerially? For example, Janet and Leo (at the suggestion of their reflection group) interviewed the former patients to see what they thought could be done and shared the results of these interviews with the patients and the reflection group.

Is this change an enactment of my theological reflection? For example, Leo and Janet designed and conducted the interviews in a way that reflected their theological convictions about the primacy of persons.

Is this enactment a new experience to be reflected upon theologically? For example, Janet and Leo presented the results of their interviews as a new ministerial experience illustrating the theology of the human person.

If Leo and Janet felt unsure about conducting the interviews, they could have set up a role play with members of the reflection group, giving each of them a description of the interviewees. This would help Janet and Leo test a new skill (the main purpose of a role play) and help the group identify more closely with the situation (a goal of theological reflection).

Theological Enactment

Theological enactment refers to what a person knows, how a person thinks, a person's theological perspective and preferences.

All theological reflection includes some degree of theological enactment because the intention and orientation of the reflection are theological. The reflection inevitably draws upon and contributes to a person's theological awareness. Something is always happening to a person's theology in theological reflection, whether it is an illustration of what is already known, an application to a new situation, or an interpretation of new meaning.

Those who do not have extensive theological training, such as first or second year seminary and degree students, carry out their theological reflection most often as a theological enactment; this is because theological reflection tends to open them to meanings they have not yet studied in the classroom or encountered in their own experience.

It should be remembered that theological enactment is enactment. It is not simply acquiring new knowledge and adding it to what is already known. Theological enactment means a person works over previous knowledge and works out the implications of a new understanding. This may entail further study, uncomfortable questions, unfamiliar perspectives, reassessment of priorities, and periods of uncertainty. In the end people claim the results of theological reflection as their own, making whatever adjustments they must, as often as they must.

As people become familiar with this type of enactment, they are able to enter new situations more attentively and more creatively. For example, one of the ministers in the opening scenario came to see the metaphor of the body of Christ as referring to the interdependence of people and systems in a community. If this insight were enacted theologically, it might mean rereading the biblical references to the body of Christ from a socio-political or systems point of view. It might also mean thinking in a new way about the minister's role in a public health care institution or the general relationship of Church and society, especially in the public service sector.

Jesus' parables were a form of theological enactment. Through them he drew people into typical life situations and confronted them with their responses which were often the result of habit or impulse (to be discussed below). Within the parable people were able to look at things differently and claim a new meaning for themselves, one which led to a fuller life. The goal of theological enactment is the same.

The following example may make the meaning of theological enactment a little clearer.

A Theological Enactment with a Journal Entry

Background

Pat is a third-year seminary student whose learning goals are to become more spontaneous and more personal in the exercise of ministry. Pat presented the following journal excerpt to a theological reflection group with these goals in mind.

Journal Entry

I visited Christie in the hospital where she was recuperating from gall bladder surgery. Several times during the conversation she mentioned that it was her birthday. As I was leaving the hospital, I thought about that, stopped, went into the gift shop and bought a card.

When I got back to her room, a nurse was there and her daughter had just come. "No birthday should go by without a card," I said, "and no birthday should go by without singing." Then we all sang "Happy Birthday."

Following lunch, I called Grace, an eighty-year-old pillar of our church, who had just returned from her sister's funeral. "Would you like a visit?" I asked. "Sure," she said. "Then get some tea ready. I'll be right over."

Analysis

I think both Christie and Grace got a lot out of my visits. Christie seemed to enjoy my surprise return and Grace said she really appreciated my visit because she doesn't have the chance to entertain much anymore. In both situations I felt that I acted spontaneously. I was just being myself without worrying about whether that's what a minister should do.

Theological Reflection

As I reflect on these two visits, I ask myself, "What made either one of them ministry as opposed to a nice visit from a friendly person?" On the surface, these acts are ministry because I am a minister. That's my role and that's how I am perceived. But that's the official, formal side from which I'm trying to move away.

On a more personal level, I believe that God works through human actions. If I can let my human love and concern shine through, people can experience God. I believe I am a minister when God works through me and that this happens best when I let God work through *me*, not some idea I have of who or what I should be.

It is still easier for me not to risk myself. But when I did risk myself in these two visits, I felt more like a minister.

Theological Enactment

A theological enactment should affect Pat's understanding of ministry. This seems to lie behind the question: "What made either of these visits 'ministry,' as opposed to just a nice visit from a friendly person?"

Pat and the reflection group pondered this question. All agreed that God works through human actions, but not everyone wanted simply to equate such action with ministry. And yet, the way the personal qualities of the minister enter into the ministry is obviously important.

This discussion led the group to recall the early Christian controversy about the effect of the minister's (moral) worthiness on the ministry, especially the ministry of worship. This was not exactly the same as Pat's case, but it presented a parallel which could shed theological light on Pat's questions.

Neither Pat nor the reflection group came to a final conclusion, but as they continued to wrestle with the definition of ministry, the following questions were helpful:

Has this reflection affirmed my theology? For example, it affirmed Pat's feeling that the personal dimension is an important part of the nature of ministry.

How can this affirmation be enacted theologically? For example, Pat could formulate a definition of ministry which would make this element explicit.

Has this reflection altered my theology? For example, Pat is now more hesitant to describe every good work as ministry.

How can this alteration be enacted theologically? For example, Pat can pay more attention to the activities which other people call ministry.

Has this reflection called into question my theology? For example, Pat is now questioning the importance of the official delegation of ministry.

How can this questioning be enacted theologically? For example, Pat can study the statements on official ministry from different churches as well as ecumenical agreements on ministry to determine how much importance they give to official delegation.

Whatever form it takes, enactment should flow directly from theological reflection, as a practical embodiment of it. In this sense it is properly called praxis and is to be distinguished from habit and impulse.

Enactment and Praxis

Habit

Habit is repetitive, unreflective action. When a certain stimulus occurs, a predictable response follows. There is no deliberate reflection on the situation. This does not mean a habit is irrational; the rationale may be so familiar that it is simply taken for granted.

Experienced ministers are prone to respond to familiar situations out of pastoral habit and let the rationale be supplied by dogma, church policy, seminary training, local custom, or personal preference. Theological reflection tries to break this kind of habitual thinking and help the minister enter each experience anew, as described in chapter 3. This also helps to insure that action flows from reflection, even if the action which results is what the minister might have habitually done.

Impulse

Impulse is spontaneous, unreflective action. When a certain stimulus occurs, any response may follow. The rationale for the response is supplied later through rationalization or justification.

Impulsive action is the temptation of an activist minister who wants to get things done and not waste time with reflection. At root, impulse is a non- or even anti-intellectual attitude. Theological reflection tries to intercept impulsive behavior, even if the action which eventually flows from reflection turns out to be the same as the minister's first impulse.

Praxis

Praxis is rooted in action and practical concerns but it flows directly from reflection. Praxis is enacted reflection. The reflection itself is shaped by the total situation, not by predetermined ideas (habit) or after-the-fact rationalization (impulse).

Praxis requires a person or group to bracket their habitual thinking and to control their impulsive reactions. A reflection group, composed of diverse, honest members, is an invaluable asset in achieving this. Even so, praxis does not flow immediately into action. Some degree of pastoral planning is usually called for.

Pastoral Planning

Planning is the translation of reflection into action with regard to a concrete (rather than hypothetical) situation. It sets up the steps and tasks needed to reach the goal envisioned in reflection. This is different from "learning theology by application," as discussed in chapter 5. Learning by application means rethinking one's prior theology in light of a new experience. Planning means putting one's theology (new or old) into practice.

Planning assumes that reflection is sufficiently developed so that a person can envision a course of action. This is a fluid process. Even after a plan has been determined, there can be surprises. The unknowns of a situation are never eliminated merely by planning a course of action. In addition, planning itself is a new experience which can generate further reflection.

Planning requires attention to a situation as it is. To be effective, it must be based on a complete, accurate description of a situation. Social analysis is a valuable tool for doing this, all the more so if social analysis has already been incorporated into the theological reflection process as recommended in chapters 3 and 5.

In the same way planning helps to keep theological reflection realistic. It takes ideals and makes them work in relation to a specific situation and the people in it. In this respect planning is an exercise in limitations and practicality but without sacrificing creativity. On the contrary planning is imaginative. It envisions options, alternatives, and innovations. It anticipates what will happen if certain steps are taken or omitted. Sometimes plans can be tested by developing pilots, models, or experiments. A reflection group can be very helpful in this respect by trying out plans through role plays or critiques.

Planning is obviously appropriate for ministerial enactment but it is important for personal and theological enactment as well. Any translation of a reflection into action calls for some degree of planning. It may consist of deciding how to pursue a new insight (theological enactment) or how to implement a new self-image (personal enactment). The plan does not have to be elaborate but it should be concrete and tied directly to the results of theological reflection.

What a minister learns from reflecting on experience needs to be enacted in the continuing practice of ministry if theological reflection is to be a complete process. Action-reflection, or thinking-doing, are not two separate functions but two phases of the same process. Without both, reflection is incomplete. A fuller account of what it means to enact theological reflection may be seen more clearly in the following cases.

Volunteer or Associate?

Description of the Experience

Recently I was appointed to a Lay Mission Membership Committee. This committee was generated by a mandate from our last synod to look into the possibility of an association of lay people to work for a certain period of time in the different missions which our church sponsors.

During the past months one thing that has stood out for me is the distinction between the terms "volunteer" and "associate." It seems to me that most people who feel called to church work today are looking for a deeper association with the Church than just volunteering.

From my readings and discussions with lay missioners, it seems to me that the praxis of this movement is way ahead of the theory in regard to active mission work and the role of the laity within the present understanding of their spirituality and call to discipleship. Projections for implementation are for years from now even though we have had direct inquiries from three individuals who wish to join our mission in Jamaica for a two or three-year period.

Social Analysis

How we plan for this addition to our church ministry would necessitate a social analysis of the past as well as of the contemporary situation. There was a system of lay associates in the past but it was based on a hierarchical, clerical model of ministry. Today more Christians are taking ownership of their skills and are desirous of giving to the Church by virtue of their baptism.

A national clearinghouse for lay volunteers averages between two and three hundred inquiries a month from people looking into opportunities for mission. The spectrum of inquiries comes from twenty to thirty-year-olds (the majority), forty to fifty-year-olds (second careers), and mid-fifty to sixty-year-olds (retired). These inquiries specify the desire for a faith-oriented program rather than a Vista or Peace Corps type of program, and are from all Christian denominations.

I recently read an article about the "Yuppies" in New York city. Many have become involved in giving time, either early in the morning or after the business day, to work in different social service programs such as soup kitchens. It would seem that this "upwardly mobile" segment of society is looking for some purposefulness other than economic status, through giving from either a faith stance or through that of social human service.

Theological Reflection

In my particular role with this committee, how do I make the distinction between the volunteer and the associate? The key term is "associate." As I see it, an associate wants a deeper connection with the Church. This involves three things: first, the individual is attracted to the specific mission and style of a given church; second, the specific gifts of the individual fit the mission of that Church; third, the individual's faith experience is widened, extending outside the person's socio-economic culture.

My ecclesiology emphasizes that the Church is a community constructed through a multitude of services. Its essential structure is not clergy-laity but ministry-community. Deeper involvement in one area stimulates deeper involvement in the other. The desire of associates for ministry should lead to a strengthening of community, and the desire for community should lead to more effective ministry. This is what lay associates are seeking. How can I help bring this about?

Praxis

I am excited at the possibility of establishing a program for lay associates in my church. Yet I have concerns in "selling" or educating the community at large about what such a program is and what it is not.

Many might feel threatened by associates becoming part of the decision-making process because they are familiar with volunteers who do not influence decisions. I have already heard opinions expressed such as, "Sure they come in to minister with us, make changes, then leave after a few years and we're stuck with what they left behind." Church members must realize that this program would be a mutual partnership in ministry and shared responsibility.

Such a program cannot be looked upon as a survival tactic for the Church. It is a temporary commitment. We must be willing to offer full hospitality to any associate who wishes to join in ministry so they may grow as individuals and deepen the meaning of their life for the period of time they are with us.

A very important factor is also to be respectful of their personal and individual spirituality. I would hope that through faith sharing and prayer together all would grow in the deepest meaning of our call by Christ to the ministry.

Many questions need to be asked and clarified and many risks need to be taken. Right now at least we are gaining direction as to how to move.

Commentary

Description

This situation presents a familiar problem in the organization of ministry: how to involve those who want to help but who may not have the training, experience, or authorization that is needed? This is often perceived as a tension between professionals and volunteers, which is heightened by issues of power, control, and status.

The minister presenting this case is very appreciative and supportive of prospective lay associates. The preference for the term *associate* indicates a greater respect than volunteers customarily receive. In addition, the minister seems committed to the involvement of lay associates as soon as possible. This could indicate an enactment from impulse rather than reflection. The minister strengthens this impression by saying "it seems to me the praxis of this movement is way ahead of the theory." Actually there is no praxis yet.

There is always a danger in establishing a program, then finding a theological justification for it. The proper procedure is to do what the minister outlines in this paper: examine the total situation, think it through theologically, and then enact the results of theological reflection.

Social Analysis

The social analysis presented here has three parts: first, recognition of the past when there were lay associates but within an overly clerical model of Church; second, data on the general trend of those who volunteer for mission work; third, an anecdote about "yuppies" and their desire for service.

Taken alone these items do not constitute a social *analysis* of the situation, but they point in the right direction. History, current data, and personal experience are valuable clues to the structure and environment within which a program of lay mission associates might be developed.

Such information contains an implicit theory. The minister alludes to this when speaking of the motives of contemporary Christians (ownership of their skills), the desires of applicants for mission work (a faith-oriented program), and the search of the yuppies (a connectedness other than economic status).

Further analysis would show whether these are simply the minister's biases or an accurate portrayal of the situation. In either case the available data should be analyzed as part of the reflection process leading to a suitable enactment (praxis).

Theological Reflection

The minister's brief theological reflection returns to the distinction between volunteer and associate and the key question: how to make this work, i.e., how to enact it? This calls for a fuller understanding of an associate (one who desires a deeper affiliation with the sponsoring church) which in turn leads to a reflection on the church itself. As sketched by the minister, this reflection highlights the church's mission and style of community, how the individual's gifts fit in, and how the individual benefits in terms of a broader faith experience.

From the point of view of theological reflection, the question of lay associates provides an opportunity either to apply (see chapter 5) the minister's theology of Church or to interpret it (see chapter 6). The minister seems to opt for interpretation, drawing from the idea of lay associates an alternative explanation (ministry-community) to the clergy-laity model which was dominant in the past.

Theological Enactment

Given the minister's obvious practical concern as a member of the committee, it might seem that this reflection calls for ministerial enactment, i.e., "selling" the program to the community at large. But a closer look shows that the actual, and appropriate, enactment is theological.

What has to be sold is "what such a program is and what it is not." In other words, its meaning, especially its ecclesial meaning, has to be communicated (enacted). From the minister's point of view, the enactment consists in getting members to see the Church as a mutual partnership in which associates make a temporary commitment and have some influence in decision making. This might be threatening to some and expose inferior motives such as a "community survival tactic."

If an ecclesiology of mutual partnership is enacted, however, it will mean that everyone will grow in their sense of being called by Christ to the ministry. In other words, the Church will benefit from the work of the lay associates just as the associates will benefit from their deeper involvement in the Church.

The minister's conclusion is an apt summary of theological enactment: "many questions need to be asked and clarified and many risks need to be taken."

Teaching Sunday School

Background

The Adult Bible Class at church is a Sunday school group of elderly women who have been meeting for many years. The members are mostly in their 80s and several of them cannot hear or see very well.

The class is usually taught by an elderly man, but he is in Florida on vacation. I volunteered to substitute for him for two reasons, my genuine fondness for him, and my desire to try something new. This is the first class I have ever taught. I should note that, although the women are full of infirmities, they are yet a lively bunch.

Theological Reflection

My method of teaching this class is not to try to pound into their heads all the great stuff that I know and they don't, but to invite them to look and reflect with me. I do bring a certain amount of expertise to the group but the members of the class bring their own wealth of experience. I try to share what I know and to elicit their responses and help them connect their own experiences with the Scripture lessons.

This method has come into being largely due to my own dialogue with two sources of experience—the model of Jesus as teacher in the New Testament, and my own experience as a student in Sunday school.

Jesus taught those around him through example, through personal challenge, and through the telling and explaining of familiar stories. Jesus' method of teaching was personal. He not only taught his hearers about the kingdom, about God, about lifestyles, but he also taught them about themselves.

My experiences hearing about God came during eight years of Sunday school as a child. Very little attempt was made to correlate the stories of Scripture with my own stories (which by the eighth grade I thought were pretty exciting). Instead, the emphasis was on memorizing prayers and being told by "Someone Who Knew Better" what it was all about. The Word of God was not an active thing for me.

My belief is that the Word of God is alive and active and speaks to six people often in six different ways. I see myself as a resource with extra information, as one who enables others to voice their own feelings and experiences in response to the Word and as a guide for those who wish to reflect more. I also have much to learn from my students.

Praxis

My operating procedure was (1) to discuss the text itself, bringing in any special knowledge or understanding I might have; (2) to invite discussion of what is going on in the passage; (3) to pick out a few themes and ask the group to relate their own experiences to the Scripture passage.

The lesson was Acts 1:4-14. I asked what they knew about Acts. G said that it was about Jesus. I pointed out that Jesus is there in the beginning, but the rest is about the apostles and the early Church. I pointed out that we are similar to this Church since we, like they, are on this side of the resurrection.

We talked about the differences between the Gospels and Acts (since there seemed to be some confusion). I spoke of how the author of Luke was also the author of Acts. G commented that that made the author of Luke and Acts the author of one-fourth of the New Testament (a fact she remembered). Often I repeat what G says because her laryngitis makes it hard for the others to hear her.

I read the lesson aloud and made some connections with the end of Luke's Gospel.

(M = Minister)

M1	So, what is happening in this story?
G	Well, it seems like they're all trying to get together.
M2	Right. We have this scene where all the disciples have come together in one room. What else?
G	Well, they're waiting for the Father's promise.

M3	(nodding) They're waiting for the Father's promise of the gift of the Spirit, which it says in Luke will come as power from on high.
G	That's what I don't understand.
M4	What's that?
G	The fact that the power will come from on high. What is that power?
M5	Well, have you ever felt that the Spirit of God was moving within you?
G	(smiles and nods) Well, yes. (She tells a brief story of feeling the presence of God and how it helped her through a crisis).
M6	So how are we like those apostles in the story?
G	Well, we are here together, we are a fellowship. And then we're supposed to witness to other people about our faith.

We talked further about the experience of waiting for the Spirit and how we are a fellowship in the class, the Church, and with those outside. Most of the women shared an experience of feeling the Spirit's presence and how they have witnessed to others.

Commentary

Background

This incident has a practical orientation from the outset. Because it concerns the teaching of a Bible class, it has a ministerial enactment in view. The physical limitations of the small group are described factually and with respect. It is perhaps noteworthy that this group of women is usually taught by a man.

The experience is important to the minister because it is the first time the minister has taught a class. This poses a practical challenge to all the ideas and theories about teaching.

Theological Reflection

The method of teaching is described first, followed by the rationale. This is different from rationalizing a course of action undertaken impulsively or acting out of deeply ingrained habit, in neither case giving much thought to the activity. In contrast, this minister has thought out the approach to be taken and bases it on a combination of theological and personal sources.

The teaching method of Jesus is primary. It is described succinctly as if everyone knows what it is. There is no acknowledgement that the teaching method of Jesus is filtered through the gospel authors and their respective literary styles or that Jesus used a variety of methods to teach, including rabbinic disputation, paradoxical sayings, and symbolic actions. The main point, however, is that Jesus related his teaching to the experience of his listeners and that's what the minister wants to imitate. This is the enactment in view.

The personal experience is drawn from the minister's childhood. The implication seems to be that the method was not effective then for children and is not effective now for adults. A more careful examination of that experience might yield some helpful suggestions for teaching this class and clarify the validity of the minister's intention not to repeat that method.

The summation in the last paragraph is a good description of the minister's goal. The focus is on the Word of God; the goal is to structure the learning experience so the Word can speak to each person in a distinctly personal way, with the help of the minister.

Praxis

The actual procedure for conducting the class is spelled out very methodically. It has the elements of a plan and is consistent with the principles described in the preceding section, although the minister remains the dominant figure (reading the lesson and asking the questions).

The exchanges with the class members are instructive. The minister seems to be committed to respecting their views while adding information or clarifying points. For example, the Acts of the Apostles, in contrast to the Gospels, is not primarily about Jesus but about the early Church. On the other hand, the fact of Lukan authorship prompts one woman to observe that this makes Luke the author of one-fourth of the

New Testament, a point received gracefully and even repeated for the benefit of others.

The dialogue shows a willingness to let people express their views and to build on their contributions. When a question about the meaning of "power from on high" comes from one of the members, the minister uses it to explore that person's experience more fully.

This class is a good example of ministerial enactment. Faced with a new situation, the minister does not simply carry out the task and then justify it (impulse) or teach the class as Sunday school "is supposed to be taught" (habit). The minister examines the situation, reflects on the teaching task, draws from the example of Jesus and prior personal experience, formulates a method, and enacts it. It may not be a perfect example of teaching Sunday school, but it is a good example of praxis as the embodiment of theological reflection.

Practical Suggestions and Questions

The following points summarize the material in this chapter concerning the enactment of theological reflection. The questions may be used to guide or evaluate theological reflection groups.

1. Theological reflection is not complete unless the outcome of the reflection process is enacted.

- Do you see enactment as an integral, necessary part of theological reflection?
- Are your students expected to give some indication of the practical outcome of their reflection?
- Is enactment given consideration throughout the reflection process or only at the end, as a last step?

2. Praxis is the embodiment of reflection drawn from specific circumstances and enacted in terms of those same specific circumstances.

- Do you see the difference between praxis and habit? between praxis and impulse? Is this difference clear to your students?
- How do you distinguish praxis in specific cases from habit and impulse? What do you look for?

- Are students expected to show that their praxis is directly related to their reflection?

3. Pastoral planning is a key technique for converting ideas into action.

- Are you familiar with the basic elements in developing a pastoral plan?
- Do you encourage students to develop pastoral plans for specific enactments of their reflection?
- Do students use members of the reflection group to test their plans (for example, through role plays)?

4. Personal enactment draws conclusions out of reflection as they relate to one's identity, self-image, motives.

- Do you consider personal enactment a suitable, practical outcome of theological reflection?
- How does personal enactment differ from introspection or preoccupation with one's own feelings?
- What signs do you look for to indicate that a personal enactment flows from theological reflection?
- Do you encourage the group to enact a shared reflection as a group?

5. Theological enactment is the rearrangement of information and understanding based on theological reflection.

- Do you see theological enactment as a suitable, practical outcome of theological reflection?
- How does theological enactment differ from theological learning through illustration, application, or interpretation?
- Are students expected to describe the effect of theological enactment on their way of thinking?

6. Ministerial enactment is a behavioral expression of theological reflection in the functions of ministry.

- How do you know whether a ministerial enactment is the result of theological reflection or a predetermined action, rationalized theologically?
- Do students identify the skills they need to carry out a ministerial enactment?

- Are students encouraged to use the reflection group in planning and testing possible ministerial enactments?
- Do students use ministerial enactments as new experiences for theological reflection?

Theoretical Background

The enactment of theological reflection is based on three major concepts in process thought: (1) the bipolar structure of reality; (2) the function of reflection; (3) the creative advance of the world.

Bipolar Reality

As noted in the last chapter, Whitehead tried to overcome the philosophical dualism of the modern period inherited from Descartes and rooted in early Greek thought. Along with the dichotomies already discussed between subject and object, meaning and truth, the one and the many, there is another dualism which pertains directly to theological reflection. It is the distinction between mind (spirit) and matter.

The separation of mind and matter takes many forms: body and soul, nature and supernature, reason and emotion, time and eternity. These categories are very helpful in analyzing and acting upon the world around us but when they take the place of the reality they represent, problems arise. This is what Whitehead called the fallacy of misplaced concreteness, discussed in chapter 2.

Whitehead's solution was to insist on the bipolar nature of all reality, beginning with the most simple, individual occasions and continuing through the most complex societies of occasions, eventually embracing the relationship between God and creation. The primordial and consequent natures of God (described in chapter 1) are one expression of this bipolar structure of reality.

Bipolarity refers to the physical and mental energy characterizing all occasions, somewhat like the positive and negative charges of a magnetic field. The physical pole consists of the feelings for other actual entities. These feelings (prehensions) either conform to, and take in, certain aspects of already completed occasions or they reject them. These positive and negative prehensions constitute the occasion's evaluation of the existing world for its own becoming (its perspective as described in chapter 5).

The mental pole consists of the feeling for the initial aim of becoming, as well as other formal elements (what Whitehead called eternal objects) which shape the content of the new occasion. These feelings transcend the mere factuality of available data and anticipate the final satisfaction of the experience which the new occasion may generate.

For the vast majority of occasions at any given moment, the physical pole predominates in the process of becoming. Even for those occasions (or better, societies) where the mental pole is more prominent, almost none of the occasions are self-conscious. And when they are, as in human reflection, the mental pole is dependent on the substratum of physical occasions to allow consciousness to occur.

The main point of this analysis for theological reflection is that there is no separation between mind and matter. Both are integral in every occasion of experience. More than that, these mental and physical processes depend on each other and measure each other's contribution to the final experience. The mental pole in any occasion cannot exceed the conditions of the physical pole or else the total experience will not achieve its desired satisfaction. The minister teaching Sunday school cannot plan a successful lesson without taking account of the women in the group.

This interdependence becomes problematic when the mental pole is highly developed, as in human experience and reflection. In this case the mental pole can overreach the capacity of the physical pole to prehend what is needed to satisfy the aim of the occasion. This may have been what the minister sensed who noted that the impulse for a new kind of lay involvement was running ahead of the readiness of members and structures of the Church to make it work. When they do work in harmony, the mental pole prehends the highest ideals and goals for the occasion and the physical pole prehends the most relevant experiences in the most novel way to satisfy the ideals.

The task of enacting theological reflection is to transform the settled experience of one event (reflection) into the real potential for a new event (action). Both events are bipolar. However, in the actual transition the mental pole of the previous event is dominant. It supplies the ideals and meaning which a new event can prehend and actualize in its own becoming. In the actual becoming of the new event the physical pole is dominant.

Thus the Sunday school teacher prehends the way Jesus taught and transforms that experience into an ideal for how to teach the class on Acts 1:4-14. The mental pole of the prehended experience becomes the mental pole of the new experience. How the new experience will finally turn out depends on the physical prehensions which concretize this mental pole.

This interaction of physical and mental poles may become clearer in Whitehead's discussion of the function of reflection.

The Purpose of Reflection

Whitehead devoted a small book of lectures to this topic. In essence he declared that the function of reason is to promote life, to help creatures live, live well, and live better. In other words reflection is oriented toward action and action gives rise to reflection. In process thought, action is always embodied thought; thought is always incipient action. Each draws life from the other and neither can exist apart from the other.

This process does not occur automatically, especially not in the human world. In fact it is achieved with great struggle and against the preponderant tendency of actual entities to wear down and dissipate. One of the marvels of creation is that despite every tendency to the contrary, life seems to push forward, upward, and outward. The explanation for this centrifugal force is reason, the mental pole of actual occasions thrusting the existing world toward what it is not yet. This movement is always rooted in the givens of actual existence, but it is always striving for the unknowns of potential, new existence.

Theological reflection is located precisely within this reflective thrust toward new and better living. It measures its vision by the givens of the actual world while grasping the aims which lure that world toward new experiences suggested by God. The movement is slow and dependent on innumerable factors but it represents a steady, creative advance toward the highest values.

Creative Advance

For Whitehead the highest value toward which all processes of becoming aim is beauty. Beauty is understood as a harmony of harmonies, a unifying of diverse entities each of which has its own internal reality. The defining character which creates this beauty is not supplied from outside the entities which coalesce; it comes from within the entities themselves. It is an expression of the harmony which their own actuality makes possible. This can never be determined ahead of time; it can only emerge along with the becoming of the entities in question.

Obviously harmony and beauty are not the only realities in the world. There are also disharmony and ugliness. These designations indicate that either the wrong elements have been assembled in trying to satisfy a given aim or they have been assembled in a deficient manner. In either case things are not distorted in themselves; they are distorted in their relationships. The more complex a situation, i.e., the more elements it attempts to harmonize, the greater the potential for aesthetic achievement and creative advance as well as for distortion and regression.

Theological reflection attempts to understand what is going on in a particular event, to see what has been brought together and how it has been harmonized. In one sense this is an inquiry into the beauty of each occasion as disclosed from within. Without knowing an experience from the inside, without being in touch with the dominant factor which makes it what it is, a reflector can miss the distinctive lesson of the occasion and settle for external observation and repetition of what is already known.

From this perspective theological reflection itself may be understood as a work of art. It is a creative interplay with completed events, reworking them to allow more of their internal harmony and truth to emerge. For this task strict logic and methodological analysis are not as serviceable as imagination, intuition, speculation, and intellectual daring. The end result of theological reflection is not so much an intelligible system of thought as an increasing sense of appreciation for the beauty and uniqueness of the events which constitute the actual world.

Only by understanding an occasion as it is actually constituted can a person learn from the experience. This is why theological reflection begins with a full description of the events reflected upon. The learning itself is not just an external analysis of an event that is completed; it is also a participation in the construction of that event by entering into the event and experiencing it on its own terms. In a process world this is what it means to learn from experience.

Theological Reflection Bibliography

Books

Bevans, Stephen B. *Models of Contextual Theology*. Maryknoll, N.Y.: Orbis Books, 1992.

Braxton, Edward. *The Wisdom Community*. New York: Paulist Press, 1980.

Browning, Don. *Religious Ethics and Pastoral Care*. Philadelphia: Fortress Press, 1985.

Browning, Don. *Practical Theology*. San Francisco: Harper and Row, 1983.

Browning, Don. *A Fundamental Practical Theology*. Minneapolis: Fortress Press, 1991.

Buttitta, Peter. *The Still, Small Voice That Beckons: Theological Reflection Method for Health Ministry*. Evanston, Ill.: St. Francis Hospital, 355 Ridge Ave. 1992.

Capps, Donald. *Hermeneutics and Pastoral Care*. Philadelphia: Fortress Press, 1984.

Capps, Donald. *Reframing: A New Method in Pastoral Care*. Minneapolis: Fortress Press, 1990.

Cobb, John B., Jr. *Becoming a Thinking Christian*. Nashville: Abingdon Press, 1993.

Coll, Regina. *Supervision of Ministry Students*. Collegeville: The Liturgical Press, 1992.

Collins, Raymond. *Models of Theological Reflection*. Lanham, Md.: University Press of America, 1984.

Farley, Edward. *The Fragility of Knowledge: Theological Education in the Church and the University.* Philadelphia: Fortress Press, 1988.

Gariboldi, Ronald, and Daniel Novotny. *The Art of Theological Reflection.* Lanham, Md.: University Press of America, 1987.

Groome, Thomas. *Christian Religious Education.* San Francisco: Harper and Row, 1980.

Groome, Thomas. *Sharing Faith.* San Francisco: Harper/Collins, 1991.

Hayes, Helen, O.S.F., and Cornelius J. van der Poel, C.S.Sp., eds. *Health Care Ministry.* New York: Paulist Press, 1990.

Hiltner, Seward. *Preface to Pastoral Theology.* Nashville: Abingdon Press, 1958.

Holmes, Urban T., III. *Ministry and Imagination.* New York: The Seabury Press, 1981.

Hug, James, ed. *Tracing the Spirit.* New York: Paulist Press, 1983.

Kemper, John and Eileen McMullin. *Time Apart: Reflection Models for Parish Ministers.* Villa Marie, Penn.: The Center for Learning, 1992.

Killen, Patricia O'Connell and John de Beer. *The Art of Theological Reflection.* New York: Crossroad, 1994.

Kinast, Robert L. *Let Ministry Teach.* Collegeville: The Liturgical Press, 1996.

Lake, Frank. *Clinical Theology.* New York: Crossroad, 1987.

Mahan, Jeffrey H., Barbara B. Troxell, and Carol J. Allen. *Shared Wisdom: A Guide to Case Study Reflection in Ministry.* Nashville: Abingdon Press, 1993.

Moore, Mary Elizabeth Mullino. *Teaching from the Heart: Theology and Educational Method.* Minneapolis: Fortress Press, 1991.

Mudge, Lewis S., and James N. Poling. *Formation and Reflection: The Promise of Practical Theology.* Philadelphia: Fortress Press, 1987.

Patton, John. *From Ministry to Theology: Pastoral Action and Reflection.* Nashville: Abingdon Press, 1990.

Pohly, Kenneth. *Transforming the Rough Places: The Ministry of Supervision.* Dayton, Ohio: Whaleprints, 1993.

Poling, James, and Donald E. Miller. *Foundations for a Practical Theology of Ministry.* Nashville: Abingdon Press, 1985.

Pyle, William T., and Mary Alice Seals, eds. *Experiencing Ministry Supervision: A Field-Based Approach.* Nashville: Broadman and Holman Publishers, 1995.

Schreiter, Robert. *Constructing Local Theologies.* Maryknoll, N.Y.: Orbis Books, 1985.

Shea, John. *An Experience Named Spirit.* Chicago: The Thomas More Press, 1983.

Smith, Thomas. *God on the Job: Finding God Who Waits at Work.* Mahwah, N.J.: Paulist Press, 1995.

Steere, David A., ed. *The Supervision of Pastoral Care.* Louisville: Westminster/John Knox Press, 1989.

Stone, Howard W. *The Word of God and Pastoral Care.* Nashville: Abingdon Press, 1988.

Taylor, Michael H. *Learning to Care: Christian Reflection on Pastoral Practice.* London: SPCK, 1983.

Whitehead, James D., and Evelyn Eaton. *Method in Ministry: Theological Reflection and Christian Ministry*, rev. ed. Kansas City: Sheed and Ward, 1995.

Articles

Gross, Joe. "A Model for Theological Reflection in Clinical Pastoral Education," *The Journal of Pastoral Care* (Summer 1994) 131–134.

Jernigan, Homer L. "Teaching Pastoral Theology from a Global Perspective," *Theological Education* 30 (Autumn 1993) 191–233.

Kemper, John C. "Doing Theological Reflection Within a Cultural Group," *East Asian Pastoral Review* (no. 4, 1992) 427–439.

Killen, Patricia O'Connell, and John de Beer. "'Everyday' Theology: A Model for Religious and Theological Education," *Chicago Studies* 22 (1983) 191–207.

Killen, Patricia O'Connell. "The Practice of Theological Reflection in Small Faith Communities," *Chicago Studies* 31 (April 1992) 189–197.

Kinast, Robert L. "Experiencing the Tradition through Theological Reflection," *New Theology Review* (February 1995) 6–18.

Kinast, Robert L. "Orthopraxis: Starting Point of Theological Reflection," *Proceedings of the Catholic Theological Society of America* 38 (1983) 29–45.

King, Eugene. "Towards a Method of Theological Reflection on Experience in Ministry," *Pastoral Sciences* 2 (1983) 33–57.

Melchin, Kenneth. "Social Analysis and Pastoral Studies: A Critical Assessment," *Pastoral Sciences* 4 (1985) 51–67.

Nelson, Randy A. "Doing Theology in a Clinical Setting," *The Journal of Pastoral Care* 47 (Summer 1993) 168–179.

Sheehan, Mary Ellen. "Theological Reflection and Theory-Praxis Integration," *Pastoral Sciences* 3 (1984) 25–38.